Oxford International Resources

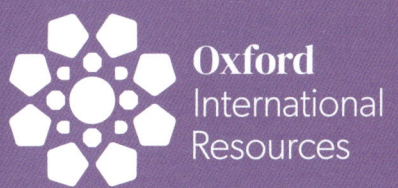

4

English

Student Book

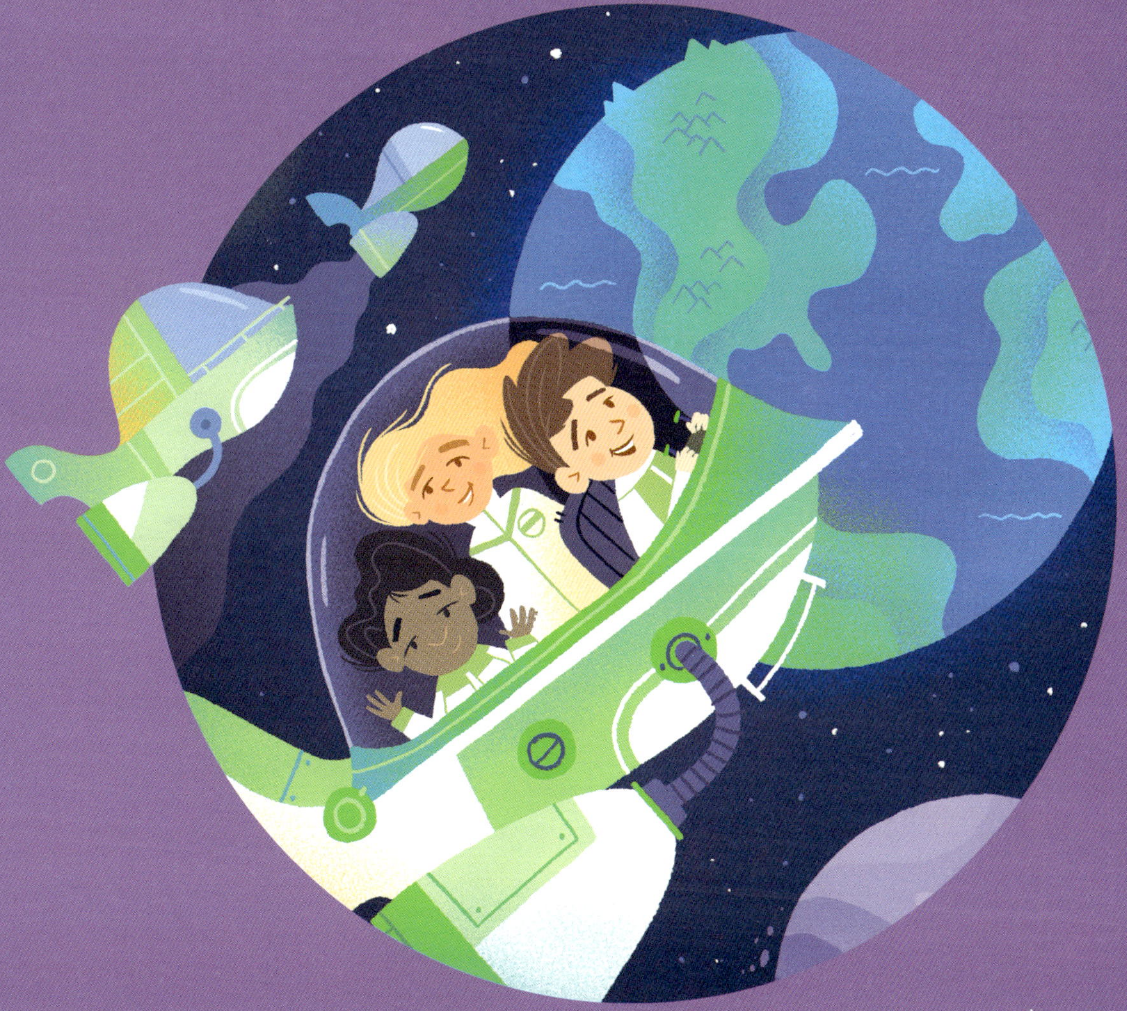

Emma Danihel
Izabella Hearn

OXFORD
UNIVERSITY PRESS

OXFORD
UNIVERSITY PRESS

Great Clarendon Street, Oxford, OX2 6DP, United Kingdom

Oxford University Press is a department of the University of Oxford. It furthers the University's objective of excellence in research, scholarship, and education by publishing worldwide. Oxford is a registered trade mark of Oxford University Press in the UK and in certain other countries.

First published in 2021

British Library Cataloguing in Publication Data

Data available

ISBN 978-1-38-201985-9

10 9 8 7

Paper used in the production of this book is a natural, recyclable product made from wood grown in sustainable forests. The manufacturing process conforms to the environmental
regulations of the country of origin.

Printed in India by Multivista Global Pvt. Ltd

Acknowledgements

The publisher and authors would like to thank the following for permission to use photographs and other copyright material:

Cover: Artwork by Dan Gartman. **Photos: p3(a):** Gualtiero boffi/Shutterstock; **p3(b):** HitToon/Shutterstock; **p3(c):** Kudryashka/Shutterstock; **p8:** Painters/Alamy Stock Photo and nodff/Shutterstock; **p9(t):** VICTOR TORRES/Shutterstock; **p9(ml):** luca85/Shutterstock; **p9(mr):** de2marco/Shutterstock; **p9(m):** Thomas Bethge/Shutterstock; **p9(b):** chippix/Shutterstock; **p12:** Thomas Bethge/Shutterstock; **p13:** Alexandra Lande/Shutterstock; **p14:** drpnncpptak/Shutterstock; **p15:** Nazarova Mariia/Shutterstock; **p17:** Ingram/Alamy Stock Photo; **p18:** Ian Dagnall Commercial Collection/Alamy Stock Photo; **p24(bkgd):** Katrina Brown/Alamy Stock Photo; **24(a):** Don Farrall/DigitalVision/Getty Images; **24(b):** Adam Gryko/Shutterstock; **24(c):** SW_Stock/Shutterstock; **24(d):** Sari Oneal/Shutterstock; **24(e):** vnlit/Shutterstock; **24(f):** Denis Tabler/Shutterstock; **p25:** StudioSmart/Shutterstock; **p26–27:** Photodisc/Getty Images; **p27(b):** REUTERS/Alamy Stock Photo; **p28:** Jill Fromer/Photodisc/Getty Images; **p28(l):** marcouliana/Getty Images; **p28(m):** Aaltair/Shutterstock; **p28(r):** Corbis; **p29(t):** Julien Tromeur/Shutterstock; **p29(b):** Niamh Baldock/Alamy Stock Photo; **p31(b):** Gary L. Brewer/Shutterstock; **p33:** Mikhail Markovskiy/Shutterstock; **p34:** Julien Tromeur/Shutterstock; **p35:** Nagib/Shutterstock; **p38:** Chris Edgcombe/Alamy Stock Photo; **p40(bkgd):** Mythja/Shutterstock; **p40(t):** SpeedKingz/Shutterstock; **p40(m):** shapovalphoto/Shutterstock; **p41:** Amawasri Pakdara/Shutterstock; **p46:** Zheltobriukh Oleksandr/Shutterstock; **p47:** Jupiterimages/Stockbyte/Getty Images; **p48:** Wollertz/Shutterstock; **p51(bkgd):** Secondcorner/Shutterstock; **p53:** Mumut/Shutterstock; **p56:** Denis Belitsky/Shutterstock; **p59:** saiko3p/Shutterstock; **p60(bkgd):** Elenamiv/Shutterstock; **p60(b):** Kontur-vid/Shutterstock; **p63:** FooTToo/Shutterstock; **p65(l):** Arts Illustrated Studios/Shutterstock; **p65(m):** Eric Isselee/Shutterstock; **p67:** Kak2s/Shutterstock; **p70(tl):** Roman Samokhin/Shutterstock; **p70(m):** Alan and Sandy Carey/Photodisc/Getty Images; **p70(br):** Gualtiero boffi/Shutterstock; **p70(bkgd):** biletskiyevgeniy.com/Shutterstock; **p71:** Hung Chung Chih/Shutterstock; **p72:** Elena Larina/Shutterstock; **p72–73:** SP shutter/Shutterstock; **p73:** Willyam Bradberry/Shutterstock; **p75:** Bernd Vogel/Corbis/Getty Images; **p76(tl):** Virinaflora/Shutterstock; **p76(tm):** Virinaflora/Shutterstock; **p76(tr):** Virinaflora/Shutterstock; **p77:** Comstock/Stockbyte/Getty Images; **p79:** Jordan Tan/Shutterstock; **p80(b):** Gelpi/Shutterstock; **p82(bkgd):** Here/Shutterstock; **p82:** Arvind Balaraman/Shutterstock; **p83:** Brian A Jackson/Shutterstock; **p86(tl):** Monkey Business Images/Shutterstock; **p86(tm):** MIA Studio/Shutterstock; **p86(tr):** Asia Images Group/Shutterstock; **p87:** defpicture/Shutterstock; **p92:** Vital Safo/Shutterstock; **p96(t):** OlgaLucky/Shutterstock; **p96(b):** Blend Images/Getty Images; **p99:** Villiers Steyn/Shutterstock; **p100(bkgd):** Photodisc/Getty Images; **p100:** Rido/Shutterstock; **p101(t):** Tatyana Vyc/Shutterstock; **p101(b):** Sergey Novikov/Shutterstock; **p105:** STILLFX/Shutterstock; **p106:** Roman Pyshchyk/Shutterstock; **p107:** New Africa/Shutterstock; **p111:** Fuse/Corbis/Getty Images;

p114: lunamarina/Shutterstock; **p116(bkgd):** Brett Allen/Shutterstock; **p116(br):** REUTERS/Alamy Stock Photo; **p116(bl):** Lakeview Images/Alamy Stock Photo; **p117(t):** CPA Media Pte Ltd/Alamy Stock Photo; **p117(b):** OHishiapply/Shutterstock; **p118–119:** Siede Preis/Photodisc/Getty Images; **p118(bl):** Hugh Threlfall/Alamy Stock Photo; **p118(br):** Nada B/Shutterstock; **p119(t):** Yuri Shevtsov/Shutterstock; **p119(b):** Alexander Raths/Shutterstock; **p121:** Lovingyou2911/Shutterstock; **p124:** Hintau Aliaksei/Shutterstock; **p125:** Dualororua/Shutterstock; **p127:** Gideon Mendel/Corbis Historical/Getty Images; **p128:** Merkushev Vasiliy/Shutterstock; **p129(t):** Photodisc/Getty Images; **p129(b):** Shutterstock; **p130(b):** jps/Shutterstock; **p130(bkgd):** LilKar/Shutterstock; **p132(tl):** Ambient Ideas/Shutterstock; **p132(tr):** Samot/Shutterstock; **p132(b):** Happy Person/Shutterstock; **p133:** Happy Person/Shutterstock; **p134:** Alena Ozerova/Shutterstock; **p136:** olies/Shutterstock; **p137(tl):** Sylvia Kania/Shutterstock; **p137(tr):** Richard Semik/Shutterstock; **p137(ml):** Peter Cox/Shutterstock; **p137(mr):** Kaetana/Shutterstock; **p137(bl):** Digital Vision/Getty Images; **p137(br):** Serg64/Shutterstock; **p139:** tassel78/Shutterstock; **p140(bkgd):** Welena/Shutterstock; **p141:** Vladimir Sazonov/Shutterstock; **p142:** Petrychenko Anton/Shutterstock; **p143:** Kudryashka/Shutterstock.

Artwork by Dan Gartman, Mark Braught, Evelyn Duverne, Milena Jahier, Richard Morgan, Dusan Pavlic, Marcin Piwowarski, Martin Remphry, Iva Sasheva, Graham Smith, Claudia Venturini, Milena Jahier, Pippa Curnick, Hoang Giang, Maribel Lechuga, and Q2A Media Services Pvt. Ltd.

Valerie Bloom: *Granny Is* from https://www.poetrybyheart.org.uk/poems/granny-is/ (*Poetry by Heart*, 2000). © Valerie Bloom 2000. Reproduced with permission from Eddison Pearson Ltd for V. Bloom.

Alison Chisholm: *Riddle*, first published in *Poems about Earth* compiled by Andrew Fusek Peters (Evans Publishing Group, 2009). © Alison Chisholm 2007. Reproduced with permission from A. Chisholm.

Julia Donaldson: *The Wonderful Smells*, from *Play Time* (Macmillan Children's Books, 2013). © Julia Donaldson 2006, from *Play Time* published by Macmillan Children's Books. Reproduced with permission from Caroline Sheldon Literary Agency for J. Donaldson.

Catherine Clarke Fox: *Who's the Fastest Jaw on the Draw?* From *Kids National Geographic*, kids.nationalgeographic.com. Reproduced with permission from C. C. Fox.

Catherine Clarke Fox: *Sea Turtle Soup? No Thanks* from *Kids National Geographic*, kids.nationalgeographic.com. Reproduced with permission from C. C. Fox.

David George Gordon: *Giant Panda Cubs give Hope to an Endangered Species* from *Kids National Geographic*, kids.nationalgeographic.com. Reproduced with permission from David George Gordon

Benjamin Hulme-Cross: *The White Seal* (Oxford Reading Buddy, Oxford University Press, 2021). Reproduced with permission from Oxford University Press.

Eva Ibbotson: *The Abominables* (Marion Lloyd Books, 2012). Reproduced with permission from Scholastic Ltd.

OUP Alan MacDonald: *A Tale of Gold and Frogs* (Oxford Reading Buddy, Oxford University Press, 2021). Reproduced with permission from Oxford University Press.

L.M Montgomery: *Anne of Green Gables* (Puffin Books, 2014). "Anne of Green Gables" and other indicia of "Anne" are trademarks and Canadian official marks of the Anne of Green Licensing Authority Inc. "L.M. Montgomery" is a trademark of Heirs of L.M. Montgomery Inc.

Naomi Shihab Nye: *Sitti's Secrets* (Hamish Hamilton, 1994). Text copyright © Naomi Shihab Nye. Reproduced with permission from Simon & Schuster Books for Young Readers, an imprint of Simon & Schuster Children's Publishing Division.

Janet Wong: *Good Luck Gold* from *Good Luck Gold and Other Poems* (CreateSpace Independent Publishing, 2012). copyright © Janet S. Wong 1994. Reproduced with permission from J. Wong.

Janet Wong: *Tea Ceremony* from *A Suitcase of Seaweed and Other Poems* (Booksurge Publishing, 2008). Copyright © Janet S. Wong 1996. Reproduced with permission from J. Wong.

The manufacturer's authorised representative in the EU for product safety is Oxford University Press España S.A. of el Parque Empresarial San Fernando de Henares, Avenida de Castilla, 2–288 30 Madrid (www.oup.es/en).

Contents

A world of stories, poems and facts

THE ARCTIC

CANADA

NORTH AMERICA

USA

UNITED

EUROPE

JAMAICA

ATLANTIC OCEAN

PACIFIC OCEAN

SOUTH AMERICA

In this book you will find stories, poems and facts from these places. We hope you enjoy them!

THE ARCTIC

ARCTIC OCEAN

·OM

ASIA

IRAN

Middle East

CHINA

SOUTH KOREA

JAPAN

The Himalayas

THAILAND

AFRICA

INDONESIA

INDIAN OCEAN

SOUTH AFRICA

NEW ZEALAND

SOUTHERN OCEAN

OCEANIA

ANTARCTICA

Unit contents

Unit	Theme	Reading and comprehension
1	**Life long ago**	**Fiction** Narrative with a historical setting *Anne of Green Gables*
2	**Beautiful bugs!**	**Non-fiction** Non-chronological report *Bugs*
3	**Tricks and truth**	**Playscript** A play on a common theme *The Wonderful Smells*
	REVISE AND CHECK UNITS 1–3	
4	**Fantastic journeys**	**Fiction** Fantasy narrative *The Abominables*
5	**Amazing animals**	**Non-fiction** Newspaper-style reports *Dolphins: Nature's Chatterboxes*
6	**Families of the world**	**Poetry** Poems from different times and cultures 'Good Luck Gold', 'Tea Ceremony'
	REVISE AND CHECK UNITS 4–6	
7	**All together!**	**Fiction** Narrative about *Sitti's Secrets*
8	**World of water**	**Non-fiction** Persuasive and explanatory text *Protect our Water*
9	**Poems for all seasons**	**Poetry** Different forms of poems Haiku, Tanka, Cinquain, Shape poem ('Sun'), List poem ('Spring is in the Air'), Riddle, Limerick ('There was an Old Man in a Tree'), Performance poem ('Fruit Picking')
	REVISE AND CHECK UNITS 7–9	

READING FICTION *A Tale of Gold and Frogs, The White Seal*

Unit	Language, grammar, spelling, vocabulary, phonics, punctuation	Writing	Speaking and listening
1	• Unfamiliar words, definitions • Adverbs and adverbials • Verbs and tenses, *past*, *present* and *future* • Irregular verbs, *to be*, *to have* • Clauses and commas • Features of fiction genre	Fiction Writing a historical story	Language choices Expressing opinions
2	• New words in context • Prefixes and suffixes, *non-*, *dis-*, *re-*, *-proof*, *-en*, *-ness*, *-al-* • Adverbs, the suffix *-ly* • Punctuation marks • Alphabetical order • Dictionary use and extension of vocabulary • Features of non-chronological reports	Non-fiction Planning and writing a non-chronological report	Expressing opinions Confident talking in discussion
3	• Unfamiliar words, definitions • Irregular verbs and the past tense • Powerful verbs • Features of playscripts	Playscript Completing a playscript on a common theme	Questions – develop ideas and extend understanding Playscript performance
	REVISE AND CHECK UNITS 1–3		
4	• Unfamiliar words, definitions • Apostrophes and contractions • Apostrophes and possession • Plurals, adding *-s* • Similes • Features of fantasy stories	Fiction Writing a beginning to a fantasy story	Expressing opinions Confident talking in discussion
5	• New words in context • Direct and indirect speech • Spelling patterns • Adjectives – comparative and superlative • Adjectives of intensity • Features of newspaper-style reports	Non-fiction Writing a newspaper-style report	Language choices Organisation of ideas
6	• Unfamiliar words, definitions • Figurative language, simile and metaphor • Alliteration and rhyme • Poetic imagery and language • Features of poetry genre	Poetry Writing a poem using a model	Expressing opinions Questions – ideas and understanding Poetry performance
	REVISE AND CHECK UNITS 4–6		
7	• New words in context • Homophones • Different types of sentences • Pronouns and possessive pronouns • Character description • Features of fiction genre	Fiction Writing a story with an everyday setting	Expressing opinions Organisation of ideas
8	• Unfamiliar words, definitions • Conjunctions in sentences • Words with common roots • Prefixes and suffixes • Features of persuasive texts • Features of explanatory texts	Non-fiction Planning and writing an explanatory text	Organisation of ideas Language choices
9	• Unfamiliar words, definitions • Same letters, different sound • Imagery and rhyme • Syllabic patterns in poetry • Features of poetry genre	Poetry Writing a poem	Poetry performance Language choices Confident talking in discussion
	REVISE AND CHECK UNITS 7–9		
	READING FICTION *A Tale of Gold and Frogs, The White Seal*		

1 Life long ago

“The more you know about the past, the better prepared you are for the future.”
Theodore Roosevelt

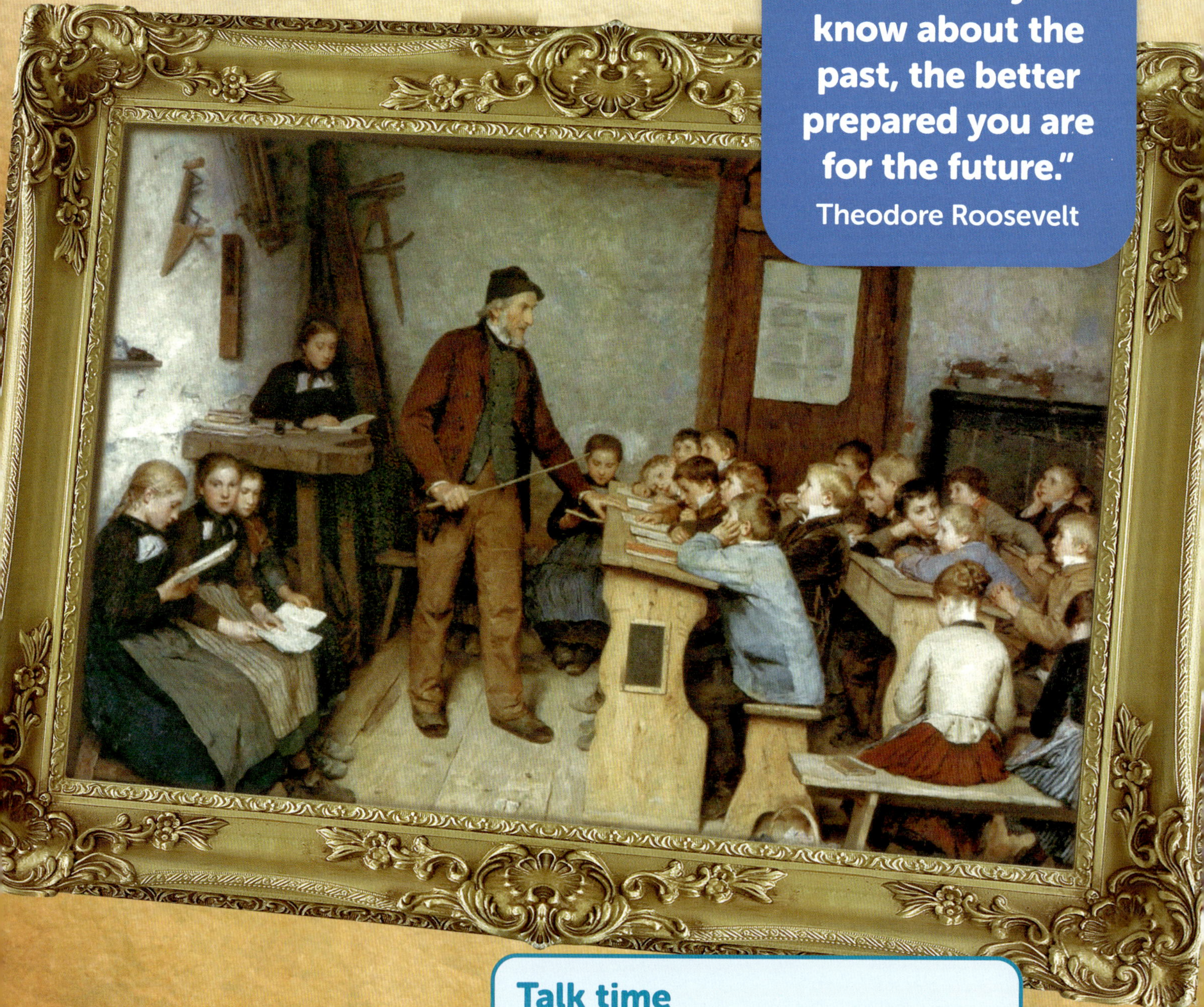

Talk time

1 Look at this painting of a classroom. How do you know it is from long ago?
2 Would you like to be a student in this class? Why/why not?

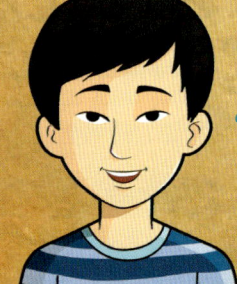

- Talk about life long ago
- Discuss with a partner
- Understand new words in context

Using words

A Make sentences using 'long ago'.

Example: Long ago, teachers used blackboards and chalk in lessons.

B Anne is describing her school. Look at the pictures and use the correct words to fill the gaps.

Today is September 20th, 1908. Today, I'm

going to use my _____ to write some sums

on my _____ . I sometimes use the _____

to help me count, too. Then the teacher writes

the answers on the _____ for us.

C Anne's classroom would have looked something like this. Does it look like yours? Work with a partner and name three things that are different from your classroom. Use the pictures on this page to help you.

blackboard

abacus

chalk

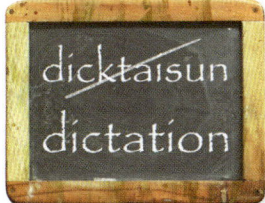

slate

Historical fiction

This story takes place in Canada in 1908. Anne is an eleven-year-old orphan, who has been adopted by a woman called Marilla. Anne has moved to her new home and is starting at the Avonlea school.

Anne's First Day

The Avonlea school was a **whitewashed** building with big windows. It had old-fashioned desks that opened and shut. Over the years, school children had carved their **initials** onto the wooden lids.

5 Behind the schoolhouse was a stream where all the children put their bottles of milk to keep them cool and sweet until dinner hour.

Marilla felt worried when she first sent Anne to school. Anne was such an odd girl.
10 How was she going to get on with the other children? And was she going to manage to keep quiet during her lessons? But things went better than Marilla had hoped. Anne came home that evening full of happy
15 chatter.

Adapted from the original *Anne of Green Gables* by L. M. Montgomery

Glossary

whitewashed covered in white paint
initials the first letter of a person's first name and surname

Comprehension

- Understand story settings
- Understand characters' feelings
- Discuss going to a new school

A **Listen and respond**

1 What is Anne's new school like?
2 Where is the stream?
3 Why is Marilla worried about Anne going to school?

B **Read and respond**

Match the verb to its meaning.

carve   to talk
manage   to cut into the surface of something
chatter   to do something which is difficult

C **What do you think?**

1 What do you think Anne liked or disliked about her new school?
2 How would you feel about starting a new school?
3 Do you think it's easy to make new friends?
4 Is this text fiction or non-fiction?

Historical fiction (continued)

"I think I like school here," Anne **announced**. "I didn't really like Mr Phillips, though."

"Anne, I don't want to hear you talking about your teacher like that," said Marilla,
5 sharply. "I hope you were a good girl."

"Of course I was," said Anne. "And I didn't even have to try hard to be good. I had fun playing outside, but I'm a long way behind the others in lessons. No one else has an
10 **imagination** like mine, though.

We had reading and geography and Canadian history today. Mr Phillips said my spelling was **disgraceful** and he held up my slate so everyone could see it.
15 I was so embarrassed!"

Adapted from the original *Anne of Green Gables* by L. M. Montgomery

Glossary

announced said something important
disgraceful very bad
imagination picturing something in your head

- Find information to answer questions
- Practise reading with expression
- Think about advice for a new student

A **Listen and respond**

1 Why was Marilla cross with Anne?
- She was naughty at school.
- She didn't like her teacher.
- She didn't eat her lunch.

2 Which lessons did Anne have?

> maths   geography   English
> history   reading

3 Why was Anne embarrassed in class?
- She couldn't spell very well.
- She had a messy slate.
- She didn't have a very good imagination.

B **Read and respond**

1 Why didn't Anne like Mr Phillips?
2 Why do you think Anne needs to 'try hard to be good'?

C **What do you think?**

Practise reading the text out loud in pairs. One of you can take the role of the narrator and Marilla. The other can take the role of Anne.

?

Anne might have felt nervous about her first day at a new school. What advice would you give to a new student starting at your school? What could you do to make them feel less nervous?

- Use the verb 'to be'
- Compare past, present and future
- Use irregular verbs

Verbs and tenses

A Look at the verbs below. They are different parts of the irregular verb 'to be'.

> was   is   am   being   are   were

1 Use each verb in a sentence.

2 Underline all the verbs that are in the past tense.

3 Make a sentence using 'to be' in future form.

B Look at Anne's story on pages 10 and 12.

Find examples of sentences in the present, past and future tenses.

C Work with a partner. Rewrite the dialogue below, changing the underlined words to make a new conversation about something else. Identify the tense of each sentence. Is it in the past or the present?

Zack: Hey Lee! Are you going <u>to the park</u>?

Lee: No, I've got <u>lots of homework</u>.

Zack: Did you go to <u>the match</u> yesterday?

Lee: Yes, <u>my team scored seven goals</u>!

Stretch zone

Write a short dialogue between Zack and Lee about a match that will happen the following week. Use the future form of 'to be'.

Adverbs

● Use adverbs of place, time and manner

Adverbs tell us more about verbs. They make sentences much more interesting.

- Adverbs of place tell us **where**.

Example: The children sat **in the schoolroom**.

- Adverbs of time tell us **when**.

Example: The teacher arrived **late**.

- Adverbs of manner tell us **how**.

Example: Anne wrote on her slate **neatly**.

Language tip
Many adverbs are one word, but some can be a phrase of two or three words. *Examples*: **in the park**, or **last night**. These are adverbials.

A Look at the bold words in these sentences. What kind of adverbs are they? Do they answer the question: where, when, or how?

1 Anne read her book **outside**.
2 It was a lovely day and the sun was shining **brightly**.
3 **By lunchtime**, Anne was feeling hungry.

B Find one example of each kind of adverb in the story on pages 10 and 12.

C Copy the sentence below. Underline the adverbs. Say what type of adverbs they are (place, time or manner). Write your own sentence using each of these types of adverb.

Last Sunday, I sat under a tree and slowly ate a delicious ice cream.

15

Historical fiction (continued)

Anne Gets Very Cross

The Avonlea school had just one class, which was full of children of all ages. Mr Phillips was helping Prissy with her **algebra**. The others were doing whatever they liked – eating green apples,
5 whispering, drawing pictures on their slates, and playing with **crickets** that they had caught from the fields.

Gilbert Blythe was a handsome boy with curly brown hair and a twinkle in his eyes. He was trying
10 to make Anne look at him but Anne was busy **daydreaming**. She was **gazing** out of the window at the blue water of the lake. She could not hear or see anything around her.

Gilbert Blythe was used to getting his own way.
15 That **snooty** red-haired Anne girl with big eyes *should* look at him.

Gilbert reached over and picked up the end of Anne's long red plait. He held it up and whispered loudly: "Carrots! Carrots!"

20 Anne looked at Gilbert **fiercely**. She jumped to her feet in a rage.

"You mean and hateful boy!" she cried. "How dare you!"

Adapted from the original *Anne of Green Gables* by L. M. Montgomery

Glossary

algebra a type of maths
crickets small brown insects like grasshoppers
daydreaming imagining you're somewhere else and doing something else
gazing looking at something for a long time
snooty thinking that you're better than others
fiercely angrily

Comprehension

A **Listen and respond**

Which sentences below are true?

1 The children are drawing on their slates.
2 Gilbert wants Anne to look at him.
3 Anne is working hard.

B **Read and respond**

1 Do you think the children are doing what they are supposed be doing? Find three examples in the story to support your answer.
2 How do we know that Anne was not interested in the lesson?

C **What about you?**

Do you think Anne was right to be so cross with Gilbert for teasing her about her hair? Is it all right to make jokes about the way other people look?

Stretch zone

What do you think Gilbert will say back to Anne? Do you think both of them will get into trouble? Write down what you think will happen next.

● Compare main and subordinate clauses

Clauses

Sentences are made of clauses. All clauses have a verb.

● A **main clause** can make sense on its own.

Example: Anne and Diana enjoyed the day.

● A **subordinate clause** must be added to a main clause. It adds information to the main clause and doesn't make sense on its own.

Example: because they played in the meadow.

Together, the main clause and the subordinate clause make sense:

Anne and Diana enjoyed the day because they played in the meadow.

A **Copy out these sentences and underline the main clauses.**

1 When the weekends came, the children liked to play outside.
2 When the weather is sunny, the family like to go to the seaside.

B **Match the main clause with the correct subordinate clause. Write the sentences and add any appropriate punctuation.**

Anne doesn't hear the teacher   when she gets home from school.
Marilla is pleased that Anne is happy   although she has a good imagination.
Anne doesn't enjoy writing stories   because she is daydreaming.

C **Look at the sentence below. It has a main clause and a subordinate clause. The main clause comes first.**

Anne is really happy when she gets home from school.
Write a new ending for each of these main clauses.
I am really happy because...
I am really happy so...
I am really happy, although...

● Use commas to show a pause

Commas

Commas (,) are punctuation marks that are used to show a small pause in a sentence.

Sentences with main and subordinate clauses need commas when:

● The subordinate clause comes **first**.

Example: **Although it is raining**, Anne goes for a walk.

● The subordinate clause comes **in the middle** of a main clause.

Example: The school, **which is painted white**, has big windows.

A Look for the main and subordinate clauses in these sentences. Add in the commas where they are needed.

1 As there were no pens children used chalk to write on their slates.

2 Anne who has red hair is sometimes called Carrots!

B Add the subordinate clauses in brackets into the sentences. Make sure you put commas in the right places.

1 The classroom was full of children. (which was quite small)

2 Gilbert liked to tease the girls. (who was a handsome boy)

C Use the table below to help you write two sentences containing a subordinate clause. Remember to add commas in the correct places.

My friend Our teacher	who is…	likes to…	at the weekend. in the holidays. every afternoon.

Writing a historical story
Model writing

Abandoned

Albert frowned anxiously. His thin arms trembled as he tried to carry the heavy bucket of water up the huge oak stairway. He had to run a bath for his mistress, but he was late!

5   "Be careful, boy!" screamed the housekeeper.

The sudden sound of her voice made Albert jump and drop the bucket of water.

Terrified, Albert watched the water go everywhere: all over the thick, soft carpet, the expensive wallpaper
10   and polished wooden **banister**.

"S-s-sorry," he said nervously.

The housekeeper was furious. "After all your mistress has done for you. Giving you a job and a place to live when you had
15   nowhere else to go!" she shrieked.

It was then that Albert started to cry...

> **Glossary**
>
> **banister** wooden handrail

Guided writing

Getting started!

- Explore stages of story writing
- Recognise features of historical writing
- Learn about characters and settings

1 In a story, the first two or three paragraphs should introduce the characters and the setting. Compare the start of *Abandoned* with the notes below.

Characters Describe/give clues about the characters – what they look like, how they move and speak, and what they say.	*Albert – small, thin, weak, tearful. Housekeeper – screaming voice, strict and unkind to Albert. A bully!*
Setting Describe/give clues about where and when it's taking place.	*Huge oak stairway; thick, soft carpet; expensive wallpaper and polished wooden banister.* *A servant and a housekeeper suggests that their mistress has a lot of money. The fact that Albert has to carry water upstairs in a bucket for a bath suggests that this is set in the past.*

2 After you have introduced the characters and setting, you need to make your readers want to read more. Albert has already had one problem: he made the housekeeper very angry when he dropped the water. Make your story exciting by creating more problems for Albert. Your readers will want to know what happens next and how Albert solves all his problems.

Writing a historical story

Your writing

Complete the story about Albert. Copy the table below and use it to write notes for four more paragraphs.

The topic sentence is the sentence you need to give more detail about in each paragraph. You can use the ones here or you can use you own.

- Sequence events in a story
- Use topic sentences
- Show characters' feelings
- Check and edit your writing

1	Problem 2 builds up the excitement	*That day, everything was going wrong for Albert.*
2	Problem 3 builds the excitement more.	*Things just got worse and worse.*
3	The problems are sorted out.	*Finally, everything was sorted.*
4	The conclusion brings the story to an end.	*Albert couldn't believe it when he opened the door and saw...*

Historical fiction

1 When you have completed your paragraph plan, tell your story to your partner. Give feedback to each other. Are the events in the story clear and logical? Is the story exciting? Does the excitement build up to a dramatic ending? Can you think of anything that would make the story even better?

2 When you are writing your story, use your paragraph plan and the success criteria below to help you. Check and edit your story as you write.

3 When you have finished writing, swap stories with a new partner. Use the success criteria to edit your partner's story. Give your partner feedback.

4 Share your story with the class. Remember to bring your characters to life and make the story more exciting by using different voices and facial expressions as you read.

Success criteria

Does your story

- include paragraphs written from a topic sentence?

- give details about the historical characters and setting?

- describe what the characters look like and say?

- use past, present and future tense verbs?

- use some subordinate clauses (some with commas)?

- Check that you have used full stops and capital letters properly and that your spelling is correct.

2 Beautiful bugs!

> "As busy as a bee."
> Traditional saying

Talk time

1 Which bugs and insects are common where you live?
2 Are any of them dangerous? How do you feel about them?

• Discuss bugs and insects

Thinking about insects

A Match the name of the insect with its picture on page 24.

fly _____   ant _____

bee _____   ladybird _____

mosquito _C_   butterfly _____

Glossary

pollinate to move pollen to a plant to help it make seeds

pests something which is annoying or damages things

B Match the question to the correct answer.

Bees are the only insects that make food for humans.

Why are scientists worried?

Bees are important because they **pollinate** many plants that we grow for food.

What is special about bees?

Scientists are worried because the number of bees is dropping.

Why are bees important?

C What do you want to know about bees? Write your own question. Can anyone in the class answer it?

Talk time
Do you think bugs and insects are important – or are they just **pests**? Discuss your ideas with a partner.

Non-chronological reports

Bugs

Millions of bugs!

Most of the bugs that you know are called arthropods, which means they have their **skeleton** on the outside of their bodies. There are over
5 a million known species of arthropods on the Earth…

We know that insects existed over 400 million years ago.

What is an insect?

You can spot an insect by counting
10 its body parts and legs. They all have six legs and three body parts – a head, a thorax, and an abdomen.

six legs

abdomen

thorax

head

What is a myriapod?

15 If you try counting the legs on a **creepy crawly** and you find you can't, the chances are you are looking at a myriapod, such as a millipede
20 or centipede. They have lots of **segments** and lots and lots of legs!

Not all myriapods have the same number of segments and legs. Centipedes can have from 15 pairs of legs to as many as 200 pairs!

many legs

many segments

What is an arachnid?

All arachnids have eight legs.
25 Watch out, however – other than spiders, a lot of arachnids look like insects so count carefully.

Pests

They may be small but bugs can do
30 a surprising amount of **damage** – in large numbers or on their own. We humans sometimes have to try hard to control them, and very often we lose.

Adapted from DK Eyewonder *Bugs* by Penelope York

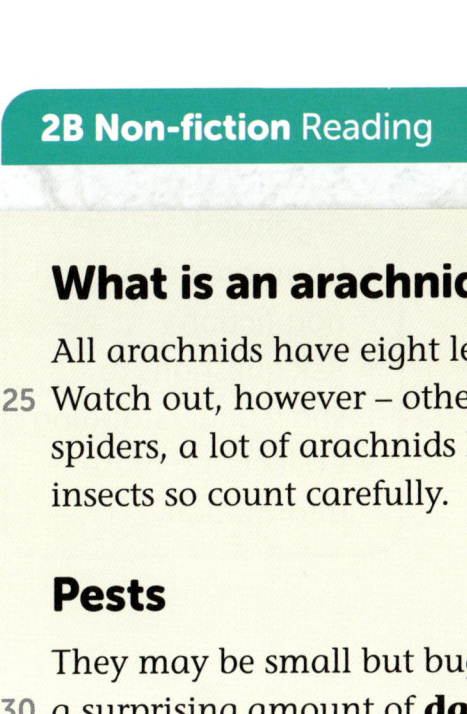

eight legs

Black widows are poisonous arachnids.

Glossary

skeleton structure that supports the body

creepy crawly informal name for insects

segments parts of something

damage harm something

Comprehension

A **Listen and respond**

1 What is an arthropod?
- something with a hard skeleton
- something with no skeleton
- something with a skeleton on the outside of its body

2 For how many years have insects existed?

400 million   200 million   300 million

3 How many legs do insects have?

4 6 8

House centipede

Male ladybird spider

Frog-legged leaf beetle

B **Read and respond**

1 Look at the photos above. Are they insects, arachnids or myriapods? Write a sentence to support your answer.

2 Some of the paragraphs have a question as a heading. Write a question as a heading for the whole extract. Explain your choice.

3 Read the final paragraph 'Pests' again. What is the main idea of the paragraph?
- Insects live in large numbers.
- Insects can do a lot of damage.
- Insects are not controlled by people.

C **What do you think?**

1 Is this text fiction or non-fiction? How do you know? Work in pairs. Take turns to ask each other questions about the information in the text. *For example:* What do arachnids look like?

2 Work in small groups. What would you like to find out about bugs? Choose one bug and think of some questions. Do some research and find the answers to your questions. Tell the class what you have found out.

Glossary

abundant a lot of something

protein an important food group

?

Insects are **abundant** and full of **protein.** Many people around the world think they are tasty too! Some scientists think that we should include more insects in our diets and less meat. Why do you think that might be a good idea?

Stretch zone

Find out the definition of a true bug. Write a paragraph with the sub-heading 'What is a true bug?'

- Revise alphabetical order
- Practise using dictionaries

Alphabetical order

A The letters of the alphabet are out of order on these caterpillars. Write the alphabet in the correct order.

Z E M Q B W D V Y H T J L

I P A F U X N C K G O R S

B Write each group of words in alphabetical order. Remember, you may need to look at the second and third letters too!

1 weevil leafhopper scorpionfly earwig
2 bug bee body breathe
3 ant abdomen arthropod air
4 spider spun scorpion spin

C Choose a word from activity B1 and look it up in a dictionary. What type of insect is it? How quickly did you find it? Work with a partner and take it in turns to time each other.

Stretch zone

Use a dictionary to try to work out the meaning of these words: zestful, zealous, zoologist.

- Practise using punctuation
- Read with expression

Punctuation

A Match the punctuation mark with its use (1–4).

1 Used to mark a pause in a sentence or to separate a list.
2 Used to mark the end of a sentence.
3 Takes the place of a full stop when the sentence is a question.
4 Used to show a strong feeling.

B Choose the correct punctuation for the end of these sentences.

1 The field was full of fireflies (. ?)
2 Where were you yesterday (! ?)
3 Come back (. !)
4 Who was that (, ?)

C Work with a partner. Practise reading the passage below with expression. Listen to each other. Did you use the right expression and pause in the right places?

Wow! Look! Have you ever seen so many butterflies on one bush? They are so beautiful! Can you name any of them? I bet I can! There's a Peacock, a Red Admiral, some Painted Ladies. Wait! Isn't that a Holly Blue? So many. It's just unbelievable!

- Understand the text using context

Non-chronological reports
(continued)

Bugs

Water world

If you find a body of water, the chances are it's filled with mini-life – but you may have to look closely to see some of it. Many
5 bugs live in or above the water and some can even walk on the **surface**.

Diving in

The diving beetle is the great meat-eater of the water. It **tucks** a bubble of air under its wings so it
10 can breathe underwater, and dives down to catch tadpoles and even small fish.

Walking on water

Pond skaters can walk on water because of thick, **waterproof** hairs on their feet. They **skim** over the surface looking for **floating** food.

From DK Eyewonder *Bugs* by Penelope York

Glossary

surface the top layer of something
tucks puts carefully
waterproof does not let water in
skim move quickly and lightly over the top of something
floating moving on top of water or in the air

Comprehension

Work with a partner to discuss the following questions.

- Understand words in context
- Discuss opinions
- Gather information
- Write a non-chronological report

A **Read and respond**

What do you think the following phrases mean? Explain in your own words.

1 a body of water
2 mini-life

B **What do you think?**

1 How do the subheadings give us an idea of the information in each paragraph? Give two examples.
2 A **topic sentence** introduces the subject. Where does it come in the paragraph?
3 Do you think the sentences in the extract are written in a formal or an informal (chatty) style?

C **What about you?**

1 With your partner, choose another water bug. Do some research to find out more about it. Write a topic sentence and then add some detail. What subheading will you give your paragraph?
2 Swap your paragraph with another pair. Read their paragraph. Is the information clear? Does the subheading fit the text? Is there a good topic sentence? Give feedback about what is good and what could be improved.
3 Share your new paragraph with the class.

33

Prefixes and suffixes

- Learn about prefixes and suffixes
- Add them to words to change meaning

- A **prefix** is a group of letters we put in front of a root word.

- A **suffix** is a group of letters we put at the end of a root word.

Prefixes and suffixes change the meaning of the root word.

Examples: **dis** + appear = disappear (**dis** is the prefix)

water + **proof** = waterproof (**proof** is the suffix)

Language tip
A **root word** is a word or word part with no prefixes or suffixes. *Examples:* happy, dress

A Match the root words (on the left) with the suffixes. Then think of more words which have the same suffixes.

1 beat   proof
2 good   en
3 child   ness

B Match the prefixes (on the left) with the root words. Then think of more words which have the same prefixes.

1 dis   fiction
2 re   start
3 non   used

C The letters **al** can be used as both a prefix and a suffix. Add **al** to the beginning or the end of these words.

ways   most   accident   though   nation

Adverbs: the suffix -ly

- Learn to use adverbs
- Change adjectives into adverbs
- Identify spelling patterns

Remember: **Adverbs** tell us more about verbs.

- Most adverbs of manner are formed by adding the suffix **-ly** to an adjective.

Examples: soft – soft**ly**   bad – bad**ly**
correct – correct**ly**

- Adjectives that end in a **consonant + y** drop the **y** and take **-ily**.

Examples: easy – eas**ily**   happy – happ**ily**

- Adjectives that end in **-le** drop the **e** and take **-y**.

Examples: simple – simpl**y**
comfortable – comfortabl**y**

Learning tip
Some adverbs don't follow the -**ly** pattern. *Example:* The boy was *good* at reading. He read **well**. Good (adjective), well (adverb).

A Copy each sentence and write the missing adverb in the gap.

1 The ladybird moved _____ along the grass. (careful)
2 The ants worked together _____. (busy)
3 The butterfly landed _____ on the flower. (gentle)

B Think of an **-ly** adverb to make these sentences more interesting.

1 The wasps buzzed.
2 I walked to the park.
3 The boy sat down.

C Change the following words into adverbs and write three new sentences.

graceful   noisy   happy

Writing a non-chronological report

Model writing

Ants

How many ants are there in the world?

Lots! Ant colonies (groups) can have millions of ants, and there are more than 12,000 **species!**

What kinds of ant live in a colony?

There are three kinds of ant in a colony. You may have heard of the queen. There are also female soldiers and males. Only the queen and males have wings.

What is the role of each kind of ant?

The queen is the only ant that can lay eggs. The job of the male ants is to mate with future queen ants. However, after mating, the male ants die! Once the queen grows to adulthood, she spends the rest of her life laying eggs.

A colony may have one queen or many queens – and many soldier ants. These **protect** the queen and the colony, **gather** or kill food, and attack **enemy** colonies in search of food and nesting space. If they **defeat** another ant colony, they take away their eggs.

Glossary
species one type of animal or plant
protect keep safe
gather collect something together
enemy someone who is against somebody else
defeat win against somebody

Guided writing

1 Look at the texts *Bugs* (page 32) and *Ants* (page 36). Work with a partner. Make a list of all the common features of a non-chronological report.
2 Look at the box below. Did you find all of the features listed here?

- Identify features of a non-chronological report
- Compare non-chronological reports
- Use a grid to plan and make notes

Common features of a non-chronological report

- Not written chronologically (in the order things happen) but in different topic areas.

- Subheadings are often questions, with paragraphs giving the answers.

- Paragraphs usually start with a topic sentence (a general sentence to introduce the subject).
  Example: 'There are three kinds of ants in a colony.'

- Written in the present tense. *Example:* 'These protect the queen...'

- Uses formal rather than informal (chatty) language, but difficult words might be explained. *Example:* 'colonies (groups).'

- Uses 'you' to make the information more reader-friendly.
  Example: 'You may have heard of…'

- Uses adverbs to move from one idea to another.
  Example: 'However'.

Learning tip
You could start your writing by making a **KWWL** grid. This records what you **K**now about a subject, **W**hat you would like to find out, **W**here you will search for the information and what you **L**earned.

Planning a non-chronological report

- Use a suitable structure
- Use subheadings and paragraphs to organise

Making notes

1 Decide which subheadings you are going to have for each paragraph.

> *Examples:*
>
> **What do ants eat?**
> **What do worker ants do?**
> **Are there any fantastic facts about ants?**

2 Next, write in the topic sentence for each paragraph. This is the main sentence that you will go on to develop.

> **What do ants eat?**
> Ants will eat practically anything. They especially like…
>
> **What do worker ants do?**
> Worker ants are very busy. In the nest they…
>
> **Are there any fantastic facts about ants?**
> Yes! Ants are amazing creatures. For example…

3 Research the questions, writing down some key facts.

4 Will you need to explain any difficult words? You could do this by putting an explanation in brackets or including a labelled drawing or diagram.

Writing and presentation

Writing

- Plan and write your own non-chronological report
- Give feedback to a partner

1 Use your notes and the list of common non-chronological features on page 37 to help you write a rough draft of your report.

2 When you have finished, read your report out loud.

3 Read your partner's report and use the success criteria below to give your partner feedback.

4 Use the feedback from your partner to write your final draft.

Presentation

In small groups, take it in turns to read your reports to each other.

Success criteria

Does your report…

- have a subheading for each paragraph? (If the subheading is a question, does the paragraph answer the question?)

- include paragraphs written from a topic sentence?

- use formal language?

- explain any difficult words, i.e. in a glossary?

- use the present tense throughout?

- use the correct end-of-sentence punctuation?

If you want to do very well…

- Use the pronoun 'you'.

- Use adverbs or adverbials.

- Use a variety of subordinating and co-ordinating conjunctions.

> **"Everything you can imagine is real."**
> Pablo Picasso

Talk time

1 What is the difference between having a good imagination and not telling the truth?

2 Watching a play can help us escape from the real world. What other activities take you away from the real world? Do you enjoy being in a fantasy world?

Playscripts on common themes

- Understand the main points of a text
- Find information to answer questions

You will hear an extract from a play called *The Wonderful Smells.* In the play, Li Hua is a poor girl who likes to stop and smell the wonderful smells from the Full Moon Café, although she cannot often afford to buy anything. Unfortunately, the mean café owners – Pang Bo and Shen Ying – do not want Li Hua to enjoy the smell of the food without paying. So they all go to court in order to let a judge decide if Li Hua should pay for the wonderful smells.

 Listen and answer the questions.

1 What does Li Hua buy in the café?
2 What does Li Hua not pay for?
3 How much money does Pang Bo want from Li Hua?

Playscripts on common themes

The Wonderful Smells

SCENE 6

(The **Courtroom**...)

JUDGE	And now, the last case of the day. Is Li Hua in court? Are Pang Bo and Shen Ying in court? ... Good. And you are **accusing** Li Hua of **stealing** from your café?
PANG BO	She took some money, sir, and didn't give it back.
JUDGE	How much money?
PANG BO	Five **chien**.
JUDGE	What do you say to that, Li Hua?
LI HUA	It was *my* money, sir. I bought some moon cakes and the money was my change. Pang Bo gave it to me!
JUDGE	The five chien was your change, you say. Is this true, Pang Bo?
PANG BO	Well, in a way.
SHEN YING	But it was a mistake! He shouldn't have given it to her.
JUDGE	Explain yourselves...

Line numbers in margin: 5, 10, 15

Glossary

courtroom room where a judge hears information and decides if someone has done something wrong

judge person who has to decide if someone has done something wrong

accusing saying someone has done something wrong

stealing taking something that isn't yours

chien Chinese money

20 **SHEN YING**   The thing is, this girl has been standing around outside the café, smelling all the **expensive** food.

PANG BO   Yes, and she hasn't paid us anything. Not a single chien!

25 **SHEN YING**   She's been stealing our smells!

JUDGE   What do you say to that, Li Hua? Is it true that you have been smelling the food from the Full Moon Café?

LI HUA
30   Yes, sir, but I can't help it. I pass by there every day. And anyway, smelling is free, isn't it...?

JUDGE   Li Hua, did you like the smell of the food?

LI HUA   Yes, sir.

35 **JUDGE**   And do you still have the five chien?

LI HUA   Yes, sir, but…

JUDGE   There are no buts about it. I have here a bag.

SHEN YING   It's a money bag!

40 **JUDGE**   Li Hua, I want you to put the five chien into the bag.

LI HUA   Do I have to?

JUDGE   Yes.

Adapted from *The Wonderful Smells* by Julia Donaldson

- Discuss, listen, ask questions
- Discuss playscript features
- Make predictions

Comprehension (continued)

B **Read and answer the questions.**

1 Look at the playscript. How do we know who is talking?

2 Who is playing a trick on whom? Explain your answer.

3 How do you think these lines from the play should be spoken? Read them aloud.

How much money?

It was *my* money, sir.

But it was a mistake!

She's been stealing our smells!

C **What do you think will happen next?**

Do you think the judge will make Li Hua pay the money to Pang Bo and Shen Ying? How will the play end?

Stretch zone

Continue the dialogue between the judge and Li Hua in the play. How can Li Hua play a trick on the judge?

Playscripts on common themes (continued)

The Wonderful Smells

JUDGE	Now, is all the money in the bag? Give the bag to me, Li Hua.

(Li Hua gives him the bag.)

JUDGE	Thank you. Now I am going to shake this bag of coins. *(He shakes it.)* Did you hear the coins **jingling** in the bag, Pang Bo?
PANG BO	Yes, sir.
JUDGE	Did you hear them, Shen Ying?
SHEN YING	Yes, sir. Thank you, sir.
JUDGE	And did you both like the jingling sound?
PANG BO	Oh yes, sir…
JUDGE	I'm glad to hear that. So, Li Hua liked the smell of your food, and you liked the sound of her coins jingling. Come here, Li Hua. You can have your money back now.

(He gives her the bag.)

PANG BO	But it's *our* money!
SHEN YING	It's our pay for the smells!
JUDGE	No. Your pay for the smells was the *sound* of the money.

Adapted from *The Wonderful Smells* by Julia Donaldson

Glossary

jingling ringing sound like little bells that's made when shaking metal things together

45

Comprehension

- Discuss events
- Answer questions to show understanding
- Recognise playscript features

A **Read and respond**

1 Why does the judge put the money in the bag?

2 Why do Pang Bo and Shen Ying think that the money should be theirs?

3 The judge tells Pang Bo and Shen Ying they have made a payment. What is the payment for?

B **Look again**

1 Find an example of some words that are in brackets and italics *(like this)*. Why are these words in brackets and italics?

2 Find an example of words that are not in brackets but are in italics. Why is this?

3 Do you think more than one person played a trick? Explain your answer.

- Perform a playscript
- Understand characters
- Use expression to create your character

C **Perform the play**

Decide who will take the roles:

- Li Hua
- Pang Bo
- Shen Ying
- the judge

Choose a director. The director should tell everybody how to say their words. Show your character in the way you move and your facial expressions, as well as the way you speak.

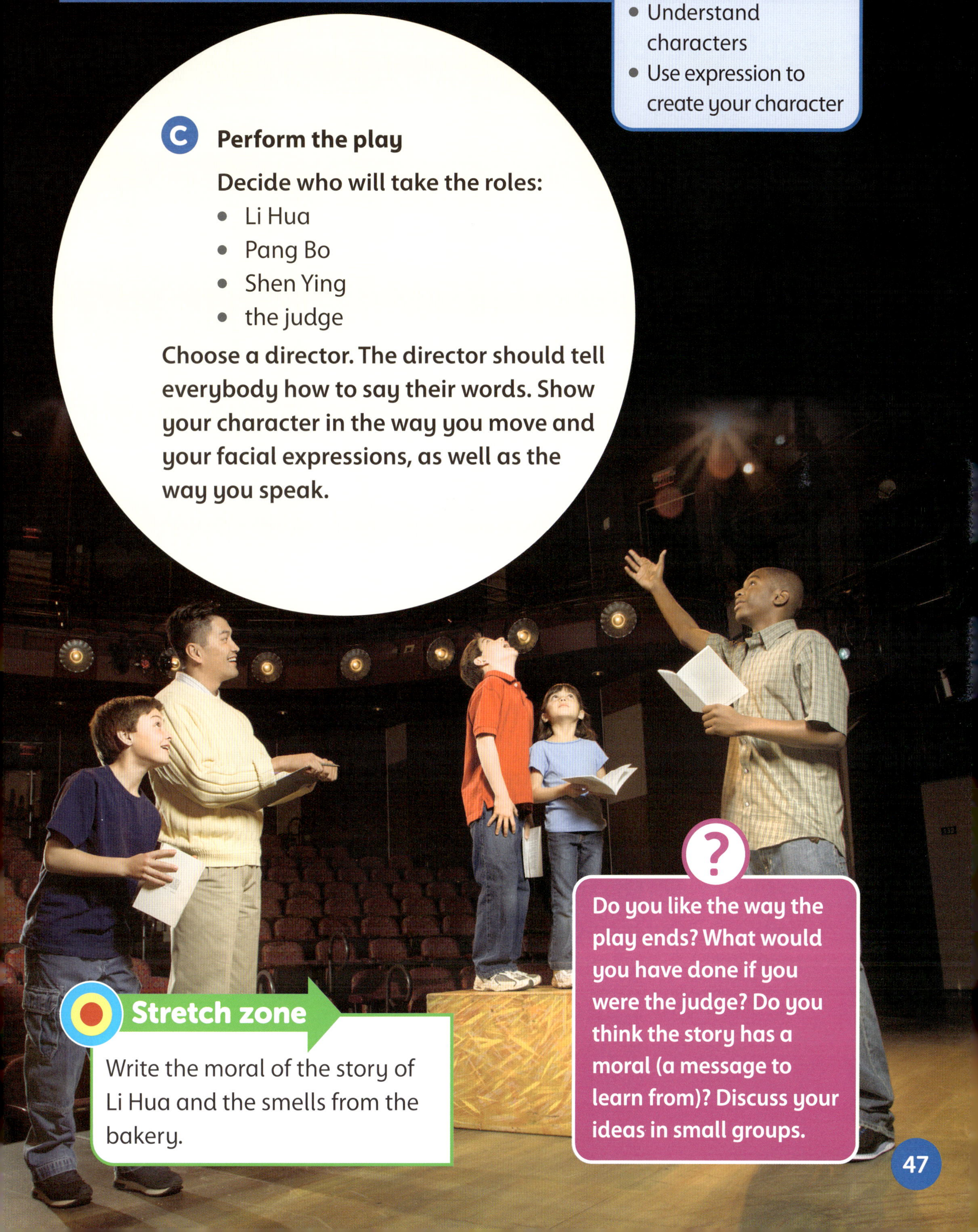

Stretch zone

Write the moral of the story of Li Hua and the smells from the bakery.

?

Do you like the way the play ends? What would you have done if you were the judge? Do you think the story has a moral (a message to learn from)? Discuss your ideas in small groups.

47

Irregular verbs

Regular verbs end in **-ed** in the past tense.

A Find the verbs in these sentences. Copy out the sentences, changing the verbs into the past tense.

1 The fox plays tricks on other animals.
2 A crocodile waits in the water.
3 The monkeys watch from the trees.

Irregular verbs do not follow a pattern.

B Match the present tense with the past tense of these verbs.

| run | hear | say | write | see |

| saw | said | ran | wrote | heard |

C Copy and complete this children's rhyme. Use the past tense of the irregular verbs in brackets to fill the gaps.

Did you ever tell a lie?

Yes, you _____, you know you _____, (do)

You _____ your mother's teapot lid. (break)

Well, it _____ only blue. (is)

No, it wasn't, it _____ gold. (is)

That's another lie you've _____! (tell)

Powerful verbs

- Learn that powerful verbs make writing interesting
- Use more powerful verbs

We can improve our writing by thinking carefully about the words we use. Try to include **powerful verbs** (more interesting verbs) wherever you can.

A Match the ordinary verb with a powerful verb that has a similar meaning.

shout	walk	hold	fly

clutch	glide	bellow	stroll

B Use a powerful verb from the box to replace the underlined words in this story.

gobbled	noticed	felt	soar
crept	remarked	landed	

One day, a cunning fox <u>walked</u> through a forest. He <u>saw</u> a crow <u>fly</u> overhead with some delicious grapes in her beak. She <u>stopped</u> in a nearby tree. The fox <u>said</u>, "Oh, Crow, you sing so beautifully." The crow <u>was</u> pleased and opened her mouth to sing. The grapes fell out and the fox <u>ate</u> them up.

C Look again at the powerful verbs you used in the story above. Which of them are regular verbs and which are irregular verbs?

49

Model playscript

SCENE 1

*(Joe's bedroom is **upstage** right. Mum enters right, shouting.)*

Glossary

upstage towards the back of the stage

MUM   Joe! The school bus will be here any minute! You're going to be late for school again!

(Joe is seen searching desperately for something.)

JOE   *(angrily)* I'm coming. I'm just looking for the homework I did last night. I'm sure I put it...

(Joe looks around his bedroom floor.)

MUM   *(worried)* Well, if you miss the bus you'll get a detention for being late – and another for not handing in your homework!

JOE   *(head appears around the bedroom door)* I'm coming!

Guided writing

- Use a flow chart to plot a playscript
- Write character profiles
- Write a playscript

Features of a playscript:

- The character's name is written on the left-hand side. This tells the actors whose turn it is to speak.

- What the character says appears after their name. You don't use speech marks.

- The stage directions are shown in brackets. They say where each scene is taking place.

- Stage directions often tell the actors where to move or how to speak or act.

- Adverbs are often used in stage directions. *Examples:* desperately, angrily.

Your writing

Carry on writing this playscript so Joe arrives at school late – and with no homework. Will he tell the truth or invent an excuse? You will need to think about the following:

- How the playscript will develop. Draw a flow chart (see left) to show what happens and how the playscript finishes.
- Who will your characters be? Choose no more than four. You could choose from: Joe, Mum, teacher, head teacher, Joe's friend, Joe's sister, Joe's dad.
- Describe each of your characters in five words/ phrases. You could draw a picture of them!
- Decide what the moral or message of your play will be. *Examples:* 'Be organised' or 'Always be truthful'.

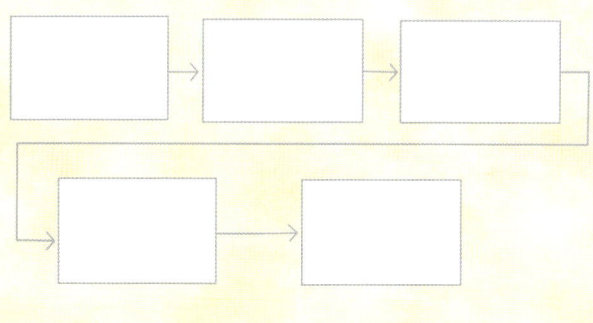

Vocabulary

1   Write these words in alphabetical order.

> skeleton   surface   slate   scrumptious   shake   species

2   Copy out the sentences below and change the **bold** words to a word that means the same from the list above.

   a   Someone had written all over the **outer edge** of the box.
   b   The weevil is a **type** of insect.
   c   Each child had a small **board** and a piece of chalk.

3   Write three more sentences of your own using the words you have not yet used from the list above.

Punctuation

1   Copy out the paragraph below, adding commas in the correct places.

   On her birthday Skye got up early. Her presents which had arrived the day before were in the kitchen. Her brother and sister who were much older had bought her some dancing shoes.

Grammar

1   **Write out the sentences below, underlining the main clauses.**

    a   The children played with boats which they floated on the pond.

    b   As soon as the school bell rang, the team got ready for their football match.

    c   In the holidays, when the weather is sunny, families like to go to the beach.

2   **Add a subordinate clause to each of the sentences below.**

    a   Bugs can do a great deal of damage.

    b   The field was full of insects.

    c   Bees can be a nuisance.

3   **Copy out the sentences with the correct verb in the past tense.**

    have   leap   be   see   hear   write

    a   A long time ago, children _____ on slates.

    b   Classes _____ big and schools _____ fewer teachers.

    c   Once, we _____ a huge spider in the bathroom.

    d   Suddenly an insect _____ out of the pond.

    e   We _____ the sound of buzzing bees.

4   **Match the questions in the small cloud with the adverbs and adverbials in the big cloud.**

How?
Where?
When?

in a moment
here
carefully
on the table
quietly
tomorrow

Spelling

1   **Use the suffix -ly to change these adjectives into adverbs.**

    beautiful   safe   brave   sleepy   reasonable

Now write a sentence using each adverb.

4 Fantastic journeys

"The moon is the first milestone on the road to the stars."
Arthur C. Clarke

Talk time

1 The picture shows a fantastic journey. Where do you think the rocket is going?

2 Do you think it will be normal for people to go on holiday or live on other planets soon?

Fantastic words

- Express ideas about imaginary worlds
- Use context to match words with meanings
- Participate in discussions

A **Below are four mythical creatures.**

> unicorn   yeti   mermaid   werewolf

1 What do you know about them?
2 Have you ever seen a fantasy film with one of these or other mythical creatures? Can you describe them?
3 What mythical creatures are there in your culture?

B **Look at the sentences below. Use the information in the sentence to work out the meaning of the words in bold.**

The **explorer**, Cassie Rickman, went deep into the wild jungle hoping to discover a lost world. She met many terrifying animals such as tigers and snakes on her **perilous** journey.

She was searching for an **enchanted** castle where legend said all objects turned to gold.

Sadly, Cassie Rickman did not return from her **expedition** to the castle and no one heard from her ever again.

Which word means:

1 a journey made for a certain reason
2 dangerous
3 somewhere magical, or under a spell
4 a person who goes on adventures and finds things

C **Think of some fantastic journeys and talk about them with a partner. What are the dangers of going on a journey to an unfamiliar place? Why is it exciting to explore new places?**

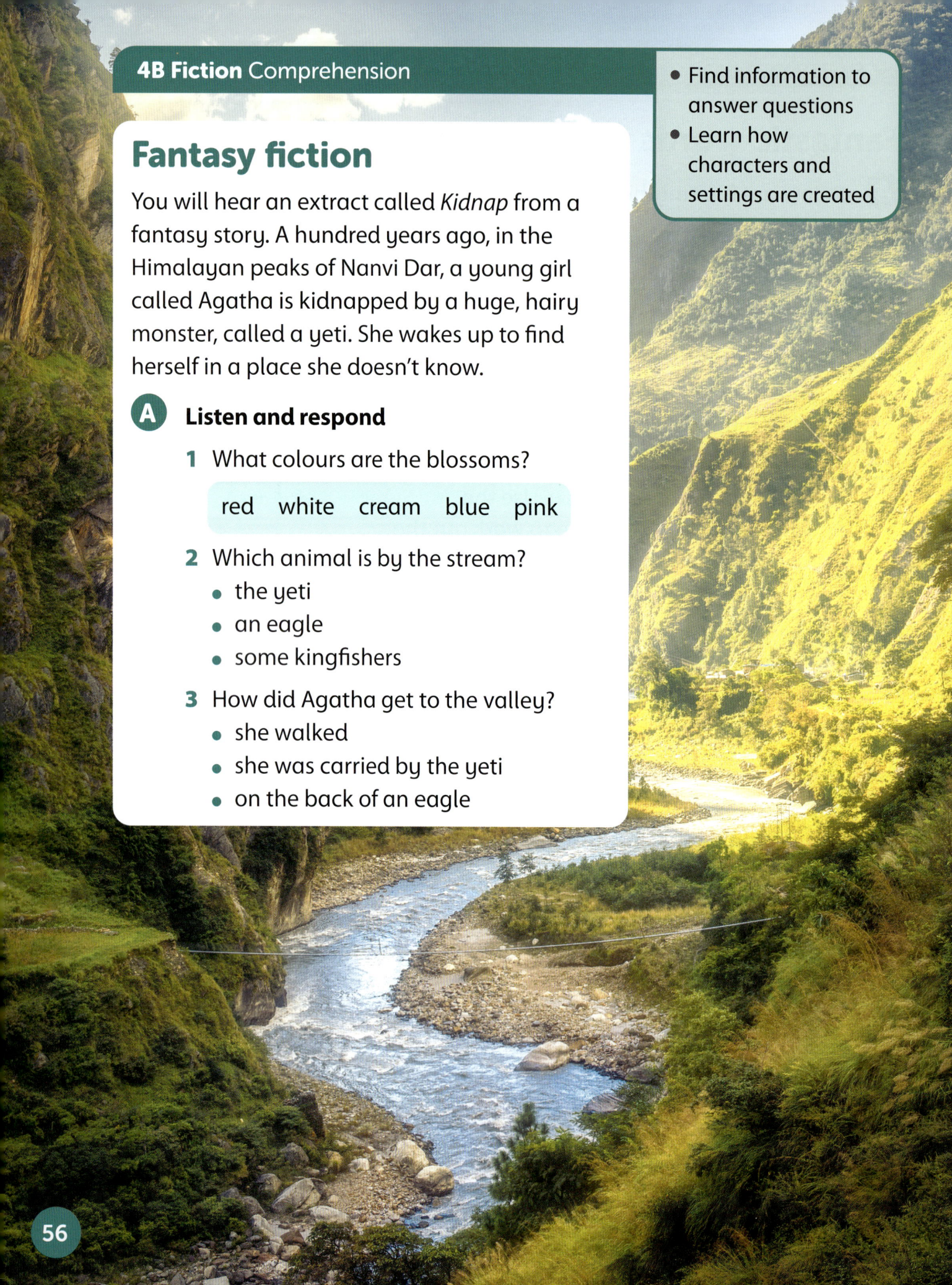

- Find information to answer questions
- Learn how characters and settings are created

Fantasy fiction

You will hear an extract called *Kidnap* from a fantasy story. A hundred years ago, in the Himalayan peaks of Nanvi Dar, a young girl called Agatha is kidnapped by a huge, hairy monster, called a yeti. She wakes up to find herself in a place she doesn't know.

A **Listen and respond**

1 What colours are the blossoms?

> red   white   cream   blue   pink

2 Which animal is by the stream?
- the yeti
- an eagle
- some kingfishers

3 How did Agatha get to the valley?
- she walked
- she was carried by the yeti
- on the back of an eagle

• Understand new words in context

Fantasy fiction

Kidnap

Agatha looked around. The air was warm, and she saw trees covered in red and white and cream **blossoms** as big as plates. There was a stream, crystal clear and bubbly, with **kingfishers darting**
5 about its **banks**. Far above her, an eagle circled lazily. She was in a valley, surrounded on every side by **jagged** cliffs. And then to her surprise… she saw the outline of the **peak** of Nanvi Dar, **glittering** white in the early morning sun.

10   "Perhaps I haven't died after all," said Agatha.

   A few metres away from her… was an absolutely enormous dark brown beast… And then she remembered. A yeti. She had been carried away by a yeti over mountains so
15 dangerous that she could never make her way back alone. She was trapped here in this secret valley, perhaps forever.

Glossary

blossoms flowers on a tree

kingfishers small bright blue birds

darting moving quickly

banks sides of a river

jagged sharp

peak top of a mountain

glittering sparkling

Fantasy fiction (continued)

"I should feel terribly frightened," thought Agatha.

20 But feeling frightened is an odd thing. You either feel it or you don't, and Agatha didn't. Instead she got up and walked quietly towards the yeti. Then she leaned forward and put her hand on the yeti's arm. At once she was buried up to the elbow in long, cool,
25 silky, tickly hair, **masses** and masses of it… then Agatha Farlingham became the first human ever to see a yeti's face.

She thought it a most interesting face. Yetis have huge, round, intelligent eyes as
30 big as saucers… Yetis also have **snub** noses and big ears and the ears have a most useful flap on them, an ear lid, which they can close. This saves them from getting **earache** in the **fierce** Himalayan
35 winds… Their mouths are big and **generous**-looking.

Best of all are their smiles.

From *The Abominables* by
Eva Ibbotson

Glossary

masses lots
snub short and turned up at the end
earache pain in the ear
fierce strong
generous willing to give things or share them

- Find information to answer questions
- Make guesses about events and characters
- Describe imaginary animals

B **Read and respond**

1 Agatha knows she should be frightened of the yeti, but she isn't. Why do you think this is?

2 Why does the yeti have ear lids?

3 What did Agatha become the first human ever to do? How do you think that made her feel?

4 What do you think is the most important feature of the yeti's face? Why?

C **What about you?**

1 Have you ever imagined a fantastical beast? What was it like? What made it different from a real creature?

2 The author makes the imaginary valley in the story feel real. Describe an imaginary place that you have heard about in a book or a film. How did the author make it seem real?

Similes

We use similes and metaphors to make our writing more interesting.

- A **simile** compares two things which have something in common. We use the words **as** or **like** to make the comparison.

- Look at these sentences:

The children ran **like** the wind.

She climbed **like** a monkey.

He was **as** quiet **as** a mouse.

The girl was **as** good **as** gold.

A Look at pages 57 and 58. Find one simile describing the setting and one simile describing the yeti.

B Complete these similes with your own ideas.

1 The yeti's feet were
  as_____**as**_____.
2 The yeti's fur was soft
  like _____.
3 The yeti's eyes were
  as_____**as**_____.

C How many different colours are you wearing today? Write a simile for each of the colours you are wearing and put them into sentences.

Example: My socks are as red as a ripe apple.

 Stretch zone

Write about an imaginary monster using similes. Your monster can be friendly or scary.

Speech marks

- **Speech marks** are placed around spoken words.

  Example: **"Hello!"** said the yeti.

- Punctuation is placed at the end of each piece of dialogue before the speech marks are closed. (Punctuation such as the following: **! ? , .**)

  Example: "What's your name**?**"

- Start a new line every time a different character speaks.

  Example: "Where are you taking me?"
  asked Agatha.
  "You'll see," replied the yeti.

- Know that speech marks show spoken words
- Learn how to punctuate speech
- Use a new line when a character speaks

A Look at pages 57 and 58. Find one example of what Agatha says out loud and one example of what Agatha says in her mind.

B Copy the three sentences below and add the speech marks and punctuation.

1 Welcome to my home shouted the yeti.
2 I am so very tired murmured Agatha.
3 What would you like to do asked the yeti.

C Put the text in these two speech bubbles into sentences, correctly adding speech marks. Can you think of alternative words to use instead of 'said', for example, 'whispered' or 'exclaimed'?

- Use punctuation and grammar to read with feeling

Fantasy fiction (continued)

Kidnap

The yeti got up and stood there, waiting, with his head on one side, till Agatha got up too, and then he began to lead her along the floor of the valley... And as he walked, Agatha saw that his enormous
5 feet had eight toes and were put on back to front.

Suddenly the yeti stopped, bent down to a little **hollow** by the bank of the stream and began to clear away the dried grass and sticks which covered it. When he had finished he **grunted** in a pleased
10 sort of way and then he moved aside so that Agatha could see what he had uncovered.

"Oh!" said Agatha. Sleeping peacefully, curled up in each other's arms, were two fat, furry baby yetis.

From *The Abominables* by Eva Ibbotson

Glossary

hollow small empty space in the ground
grunted low, short sound

Comprehension

- Learn how to make setting and characters realistic
- Express an opinion about the yeti
- Make a prediction

A **Listen and respond**

1 How many toes does a yeti have on each foot?
2 What else is unusual about a yeti's feet?
3 Where does the yeti stop?
4 Why does the yeti stop?

B **Read and respond**

Use phrases from the story to help with your answers.

1 How does the author let us know that the yeti is patient?
2 How do we know that the yeti has big feet?
3 How do you know that Agatha is surprised to find the babies?
4 Why do you think the baby yetis are covered in dried grass and sticks?

C **What about you?**

The yeti and Agatha have started to become friends. Talk with a partner about the characters and how their friendship makes you feel. Describe an adventure that the yetis and Agatha might have together.

63

The apostrophe – contractions

Apostrophes are used in **contractions**. This is when words are shortened by leaving out a letter. The apostrophe is there to show us that a letter is missing.

Example: **She's** always late. (**She is** always late.)

We usually use contractions when we are speaking.

"**That's** funny. I **can't** see the princess anywhere," said the prince.

A Match the contractions (left) to the words (right).

who's	let us
you're	they will
they'll	you are
let's	who is

B Rewrite these sentences using contractions.

1 Who is going to arrive first?
2 The explorers did not know the way.
3 The yeti can not be found.

C Write three sentences of your own containing one or two contractions. With a partner, read out your sentences. Can your partner identify all the contracted words? Can you identify your partner's contracted words?

Stretch zone

Make a list of more contractions and use them in a sentence.

The apostrophe – possession

Apostrophes are also used to show us that something belongs to someone. This is called **possession**.

Example: Agatha put her hand on the yeti**'s** arm.

The owner of the arm is the yeti. The apostrophe always comes after the owner.

- Learn about apostrophes for possession
- Learn that apostrophes for possession and contraction are different
- Know that an apostrophe isn't needed for a plural noun

A Write these sentences, underlining the owner and adding the apostrophe.

1 The childs coat was on the seat.
2 The horses ate the yetis food.
3 She came in her fathers car.

B Rewrite these phrases using an apostrophe + s (**'s**).

1 The carrots of the rabbit.
2 The tail of the cat.
3 The edge of the water.

Learning tip
Remember, if you are adding an **s** just to make a noun plural, you do not add an apostrophe, i.e. cat – cats.

C In pairs, write a list of people's names that begin with each letter of the alphabet. For each name, add an object which also begins with the same letter. Use the possessive apostrophe to show what each person owns.
Example: Amy's apples.

Writing a fantasy story

Model writing

Malik was sitting at home. He was bored and staring out of the window at the endless rain.

Then, as lightning flashed across the afternoon sky, he suddenly shouted out, "I want an adventure!"

Well, who could have guessed what happened next?

There was an angry bang, a thick cloud of smoke and a large whoosh.

Now here he was, in the middle of a forest, next to a broken signpost saying, 'Welcome to Alania'. And, what's more, there was a note pinned underneath saying, 'Help needed!'

Malik had wanted an adventure, but now, as the sky darkened and odd noises filled the air, he wasn't quite so sure...

Guided writing

Look at pages 57, 58 and 62 again. Work with a partner. Make a list of all the typical features of a fantasy story.

Then look at the list below. Did you find some of the features listed here?

- A real-life character is placed in a fantasy world.

- There can be strange talking plants, talking animals, fantastical talking beasts and even talking monsters!

- Some beasts can be invented (not real), with made-up names. Or there can be dragons, goblins, elves and fairies.

- There might also be a prince or princess, or perhaps an older, wiser character.

- There is often a battle between good and evil. Sometimes, the fantasy world is in danger and the hero or heroine need to help to save it.

- Doors, rings and secret messages can play an important part in the story.

Making notes

Plan your own beginning to a fantasy story. Start by making a story plan like the one below. Don't forget to stop your story at an exciting point so that the reader has to guess what happens next!

- Plan your story by making notes
- Include features of fantasy writing
- Consider how to start your story

1 List some 'fantasy' features you are going to include.

Examples: a deserted castle, a five-headed monster, a talking plant.

2 List the three main characters in your story and write some information about them.

Examples: a lonely princess, a scary beast with one eye, a green goblin.

3 Write some of the words the characters are going to say.

Example: "Please help! A monster is chasing me!"

4 Decide how many paragraphs you are going to have, and write one sentence to sum up what is going to happen in each paragraph.

Example: The princess runs through the forest and arrives at an old, deserted castle.

- Write your own fantasy story
- Use correct punctuation and grammar
- Give feedback to a partner

Your writing

Writing

1 Use your notes to tell your partner the beginning of your story. Listen to your partner's story beginning. Give each other feedback.

2 Use your notes, the success criteria and the feedback from your partner to write your story beginning. When you are finished, read your story out loud to yourself. Has your description of the setting and characters brought them to life? Do the events make sense? Have you achieved all the success criteria?

3 Swap your story beginning with a new partner. Read your partner's story and use the success criteria to give your partner feedback.

4 Share your story beginning with the class.

Learning tip

You can start a story in lots of different ways. You could use an expression of time: **One fine day**…
Or start with some action:
Bella ran as she had never run before…

Success criteria

Does your story

- include some fantasy features?

- include at least three characters?

- have paragraphs that build up tension / excitement?

- stop at an exciting and tense point?

- use apostrophes for contractions correctly?

- use verbs in the right tense?

- use some subordinating and co-ordinating conjunctions? (*because, as, if, so, although*)

- Check that you have used full stops and capital letters properly and that your spelling is correct.

SAVE US

"I love painting with a palette full of words."
Michael J. Budnicki

Talk time

1 Look at this poster. Do you think it is effective? Explain why.

2 Why do you think the artist chose these pictures and used only two words?

- Use clues and a definition to work out a word
- Join in discussions

What's the story?

A Add the missing vowels to the words below to complete the definitions of words connected with newspapers.

Example: n**e**ws: information about recent events

1 r_p_rt: a description of an event
2 c_l_mn: a piece of writing that appears regularly in a newspaper
3 h_ _dl_n_: the title of a newspaper article
4 j_ _rn_l_st: a person who writes for newspapers

Glossary

captive kept in a cage or closed space
extinct not existing anymore

B Match the headlines with the first lines of these news stories.

THE NEWS **BABY BOOM!**

NEWS CIRCLE **SEA TURTLE SOUP? NO THANKS!**

DAILY NEWS **WHO'S THE FASTEST JAW ON THE DRAW?**

Su Lin, the giant panda… is one of 19 **captive** pandas to turn a year old.

Sea turtles have been on Earth for millions of years, but they are in danger of going **extinct**.

Which animal has the fastest snapping jaw?

C With a partner, choose one of the news stories above. What might the rest of the story say?

Newspaper-style reports

DOLPHINS: NATURE'S CHATTERBOXES

Dolphin conversations

I bet you chat to your friends and family all the time, don't you? Well, did you know that humans aren't the only **mammals** who chat to each other? Dolphins have been recorded having 'conversations'
5 with each other too. There is evidence that they pause, listen to each other, and then respond.

Starting from birth, dolphins are very **vocal**. Evidence suggests that they may learn to talk in a similar way as human babies. They practise lots of different sounds
10 until they learn how to use them to communicate.

There have been studies done on captive dolphins, where a mother and baby in separate tanks seemed to communicate using a sort of dolphin telephone!

What do dolphins talk about?

Apparently dolphins can talk about anything from
15 "There's fish over there" to telling other dolphins how they're feeling, like if they want to play or if they're feeling threatened. The challenge is for scientists to 'crack the code' and understand what they're talking about.

20 Denise Herzing runs the Wild Dolphin Project, which studies wild dolphin behaviour and communication. She uses something called a **hydrophone** to record the dolphins. Denise says that dolphins have names for each other. "The signature whistle is a whistle
25 that's specific to an individual dolphin, and it's like a name. You'd find this whistle when mothers and **calves** are **reuniting**."

Glossary

mammals animals which give birth to live young and feed them with milk

vocal using the voice

hydrophone underwater recording device (hydro = water; phone = sound or voice)

calves baby dolphins

reuniting coming back together

Can we chat to dolphins?

Denise has been working on communicating with the dolphins. Using sounds based on dolphins' squawks, whistles and clicks, she has been teaching the dolphins to associate a certain sound with a toy, like a rope or scarf. She has also been working on calling a certain dolphin using a recording of its signature whistle.

So, while it's unlikely that we'll ever be able to have a conversation with a dolphin, they may be able to respond to simple instructions in a similar language to their own.

Dolphin sounds
- chirp
- click
- squawk
- squeak
- whistle

73

- Locate information to answer questions
- Discuss language and organisation

Comprehension

A **Listen and respond**

1 Scientists are trying to find out...
   - how dolphins make the noises
   - what the noises mean
   - whether dolphins can chat to other marine animals.
2 A signature whistle is…
   - an alarm signal
   - an individual dolphin's name
   - an invitation to play.

B **What do you think?**

Use information from the newspaper report to explain your answers.

1 Explain why the report has the headline 'Dolphins: Nature's Chatterboxes'.
2 Do you think this story belongs on the front page of a newspaper? If not, where?
3 The newspaper report uses both formal and informal (chatty) language. Why do you think it uses these different styles?

• Discuss pros and cons of captive animals

C **What about you?**

Scientists have studied both wild and captive dolphins. How do you feel about animals being kept captive – for example, in zoos?

Some people think wild animals belong in the wild. Other people think that we need to keep some animals captive to learn more about them. What are the advantages and disadvantages of places like zoos? Have a class discussion on this topic.

Stretch zone

Write a list of the pros and cons of creating national parks to protect wildlife.

Adjectives – comparative and superlative

- Learn about comparative and superlative adjectives

When we compare nouns, we often use **comparative** and **superlative** adjectives.

big   **bigger**   **biggest**

We add **-er** or **more** to make the **comparative** and **-est** or **most** to make the **superlative**.

A Sort these words and phrases into adjectives, comparatives and superlatives.

red   sleepiest   more beautiful
laziest   quicker   old

B Which words are missing?

Adjective	Comparative	Superlative
large	larger	
busy		busiest
	darker	darkest
comfortable	more comfortable	
	gentler	

Language tip
Be careful! Although we usually just add **-er** or **-est**, the spelling sometimes changes a bit.
Example:
noisy   noisier   noisiest

C Write a sentence for each of the missing words above.

Adjectives – intensity

- Use adjectives of intensity to make writing interesting
- Learn that adding -ish makes adjectives less intense

Using adjectives that show different amounts of **intensity** (strength) can make our writing more accurate and interesting. Adding the suffix **-ish** to an adjective makes it less intense.

Example: She had a **smallish** cake.

We can use a different adjective to make something seem more intense.

Example: She had a **big** cake.

She had a **huge** cake.

A Look at these sentences. Think of a more intense adjective to fill in the spaces.

1 The baby monkey was small.
The monkey was _____.

2 The boy felt sad.
The boy felt _____.

3 The mouse was frightened.
The mouse was _____.

B Put these adjectives in order of intesity, starting with the coldest.

scorching   warmish   mild

cold   freezing   hot

C Think of some more adjectives that describe temperature. Where would they fit in your list? Can you include some similes?

Example: as hot as a burning fire.

Moko the Dolphin Saves the Day!

Moko the bottlenose dolphin is a regular visitor around the coast of North Island, New Zealand. But yesterday she surprised everyone by rescuing two whales that were stuck on the beach.

5   Local people tried to push the whales back into the sea at Mahia Beach, but were unsuccessful.

Finally, the local **conservation officer**, Mike Smith, said perhaps it was time to think about
10 killing the whales **humanely** to stop their suffering.

It was at this exact moment that Moko the dolphin arrived!

''Moko just came flying through the water and pushed in between us and the whales,''
15 said Juanita Symes, one of the **rescuers**. ''She obviously heard their **distress calls** and came to help.''

Juanita explained that Moko and the whales chirped to each other, then Moko led the the whales
20 through a narrow **channel** out towards the safety of the sea. ''It was amazing!'' she added.

The whales have not been seen since, but Moko continues to visit the beach regularly – much to the delight of visitors!

Glossary

conservation officer person whose job it is to protect wildlife and the environment

humanely kindly

rescuers people who save others from danger

distress calls cries for help

channel length of water

Comprehension

A **Read and respond**

1 Which phrase (lines 1–5) tells us that Moko was often seen in the seas around North Island?

2 Which phrase (lines 13–17) tells us the whales were trying to say they were in trouble?

3 Which word (lines 22–24) means happiness?

B **What do you think?**

Use information from the newspaper report to support your answer.

1 Was Mike Smith being unkind when he suggested killing the whales?

2 Did Moko and the whales understand each other?

3 Do you think the rescue was amazing? Why?

4 Newspapers often contain both **fact** and **opinion**. Which parts of the newspaper report are fact and which are opinion?

C **What about you?**

Why do you think newspapers often mix fact and opinion?

- Understand new words in context
- Use knowledge of grammar and punctuation to understand the report
- Learn the difference between fact and opinion

Stretch zone

Imagine you are designing a new magazine. What headline would you put on the front of the first issue that would persuade people to buy it?

Indirect speech

- **Direct speech** uses the exact words someone says and includes them in speech marks.

  Example: "I'm going out," said Marek.

- **Indirect speech** gives the same information without quoting the speaker.

  Example: Marek said he was going out.

- In indirect speech, the **present simple tense** usually changes to the **past simple**.

  Example: "There <u>are</u> whales on the beach," announced Max.

  Max announced that there <u>were</u> whales on the beach.

- In indirect speech, the **present continuous tense** usually changes to the **past continuous**.

  Example: "Leo <u>is swimming</u>," explained Aisha.

  Aisha explained that Leo <u>was swimming</u>.

- Compare direct and indirect speech
- Write indirect speech
- Use the correct punctuation for direct speech

Learning tip
Indirect speech is also known as reported speech.

A Change the direct speech to indirect speech.

1 "My favourite sport is cricket," announced Jasmine.
2 "It's too late to watch television, Mohamed," said Mum.

B Change the indirect speech to direct speech.

1 Lyra said she was reading her school book.
2 Harry whispered that he was reading.

Spellings, verbs and patterns

- Find spelling patterns
- Work out spelling rules
- Apply the rules to avoid mistakes

Many words take **-s** and **-ing** for the present and **-ed** for the past.

Example:

	Present	Past
jump	jump**s**, jump**ing**	jump**ed**

But if the ending is different, the rule changes!

A Here is what happens if the word ends with an 'e'.

	Present	Past
dance	dances, dancing	danced

Now write a similar chart for 'smile' and 'glance'.

B Here is what happens if the verb has a consonant followed by 'y'.

	Present	Past
fry	fries, frying	fried

What has happened to the 'y'?

C When the verb has a short vowel, the consonant doubles.

	Present	Past
hug	hugs, hugging	hugged

Make a list of more verbs like this.

Learning tip
Remember! If the verb ends in a hissing or buzzing sound it needs **-es** in the present.
The bee buzz**es**!
The snake hiss**es**!

Writing a newspaper-style report

Model writing

- Discuss features of non-fiction
- Identify features of a newspaper report
- Think about catchy headlines

School Children Earn Their Stripes!

Students in Sumatra, Indonesia, have decided that they are not happy to sit back and watch the tiger become extinct in their lifetimes so they have come up with their own scheme to save this beautiful beast.

They have created the wonderfully named 'Earn your stripes' society, with the one aim of getting young people to work together to save tigers.

"Tigers are on the edge of extinction," says society member, Arif. "There is a need for everyone to be aware of the importance of tigers."

He went on to explain that he wanted young people of the future to have the same chance as him to see tigers in their natural habitats and not locked away in zoos.

So far, the society has 1,723 members and its membership is growing every day. If you're interested in earning your stripes, you do not have to live in Sumatra to become a member. You can become an overseas member and receive regular updates.

It's an excellent cause so why not join today? If we all work together, we can make a difference to the future of tigers!

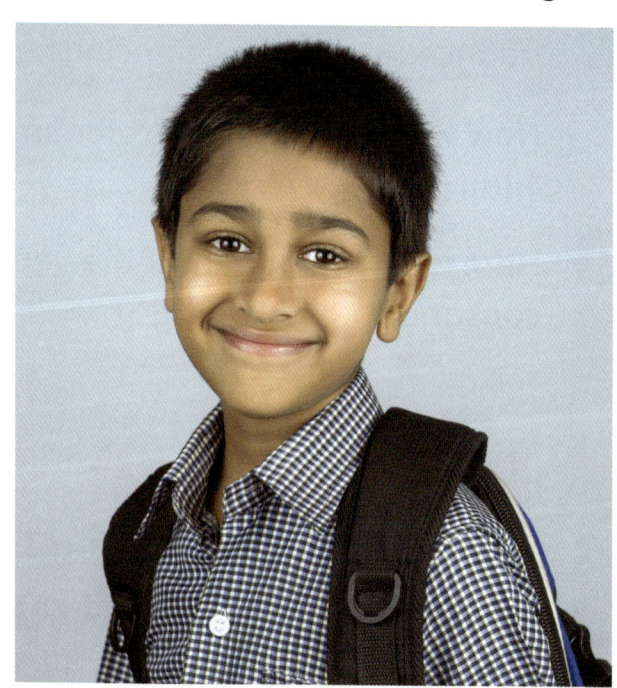

'Earn your stripes' member, Arif

Look at this model newspaper report and the reports on pages 72–73 and 78. Make a list of all the common features of newspaper reports.

Guided writing

Common features of a newspaper report

A CATCHY HEADLINE

that makes the reader want to read the report!

The first paragraph sums the story up.

Presented in paragraphs.

May include both fact and opinion.

Quotations from people involved give more information.

May include indirect speech summarising information from people involved.

May have a chatty or a more formal style.

The story always finishes with some reference to what happens afterwards.

- Plan a newspaper report
- Include newspaper report features

Making notes

Write an eye-catching headline for each of the following report ideas about brave animals.

1 A cat helps a family to escape from a house fire.
2 A dolphin saves a drowning child.
3 A dog rescues a group of climbers from a snowy mountain.

Choose one of the ideas. With a partner, work out the details and how the animal saved the people.

Make a plan of your newspaper report. You can use a mind map, flow chart, table or a list to record your ideas.

You will need to include:

- An eye-catching headline that tells the reader what the story is about.
- A summary of the story in the first paragraph.
- Quotations from at least two people. Remember to add speech marks at the beginning and end and use a capital letter at the beginning of a quotation.
- A reference in the last paragraph to what happens afterwards. The reader should feel that any problems have been solved!

Learning tip
Remember: A headline might often be a **pun** ('Lost and Hound') or use **alliteration** ('Cool Cat!'). Headlines are not written in full sentences.

84

Your writing

Writing a newspaper report

- Give feedback to a partner
- Write your own newspaper report
- Use correct punctuation and grammar

1 Use your plan to help you tell a new partner about your newspaper report. Listen to your partner's newspaper report. Give each other feedback. Is the headline interesting? Does the first paragraph sum up the whole story? Have quotations been included? Does the story make sense?

2 Use your plan, the success criteria and the feedback from your partner to write your newspaper report.

3 When you are finished, read your story out loud to yourself. Have you achieved all the success criteria?

4 Display your report for other students to read.

Learning tip
You could draw a picture to illustrate your report or find a suitable photo on the internet.

Success criteria

Does your report

- have a catchy headline?

- have at least two paragraphs?

- sum up the story in the first paragraph?

- have at least two quotations?

- have quotation marks around any direct speech?

- describe what happens afterwards in the final paragraph?

- use capital letters for names and places?

- Check that you have used full stops and capital letters properly and that your spelling is correct.

6 Families of the world

Talk time

1 Where do you think the people in the photographs come from or live? Imagine their lives.

2 Think about your own grandparents and family. Were they born somewhere different from you?

"Family is a life jacket in the stormy sea of life."

J.K. Rowling

Exploring different cultures

A Use the glossary to help you explain what the following statements mean.

1 Nadia was born in the United Kingdom but her **roots** are in Egypt.
2 Toronto is a city with lots of different **cultures**.
3 We all share a common **ancestor**.

B Work with a partner and write the questions to go with these answers.

1 I live with my mum, dad, two brothers and grandad.
2 I am American but my grandad was born in Kenya.
3 I call my grandad 'Babu'.

C Imagine you are interviewing a person from one of the photographs on page 86. What questions might you ask to find out how their life is different to yours?

- Respect other traditions and cultures
- Understand new words in context
- Ask and answer questions
- Use appropriate vocabulary for an interview

Glossary

roots person's family or background

culture the language, traditions, food, art and music of a group of people

ancestor member of your family who lived many years ago

Poems from different times and cultures

Janet Wong is a children's author and a poet. She was born in the United States, but her family are from South Korea and China. She grew up in a modern city, but her family had very old traditions (ways of doing things).

Janet Wong describes how she was given 'good luck gold' when she was one month old.

Good Luck Gold

When I was a baby
one month old,
my grandparents gave me
good luck gold:
5 a golden ring
so soft it bends,
a golden necklace
hooked at the ends,
a golden bracelet
10 with coins that say
I will be rich
and happy someday.

I wish that gold
would work real soon.
15 I need my luck
this afternoon.

Janet S. Wong

When she was older, Janet Wong took part in another important family tradition: serving tea to her grandfather.

A ceremony is a formal activity that you might do on a special occasion.

Tea Ceremony

"This tea costs sixty dollars a pound,"
Grandfather announces, and **grunts**
as I begin to pour.
This is a **signal**
5 for Mother
to look at my free hand,
a glance that lasts
long enough to **scold**:
Two hands!

10 Like a puppet
I lift my left hand,
answering her silent **command**
to hold the lid down,
while my right hand
15 tips the teapot
toward Grandfather
in a slow, deep bow.

Two hands!
I feel all eyes watching
20 as I **cradle**
the old heat-cracked cup
in soft hands of **respect**,
holding it out to Grandfather
like an **offering**
25 to the gods.

Janet S. Wong

Glossary

grunts low, short sounds
signal sign
scold tell someone off
command order or instruction
cradle hold carefully
respect admire and look up to someone
offering something that is offered or given as a gift

Comprehension

A Read and respond

Find the two sentences below which describe 'Good Luck Gold'. Then find the two sentences that describe 'Tea Ceremony'.

1 The poet talks about a ceremony from a different culture.
2 The poem describes an important family tradition that is said to bring luck.
3 The poem describes the giving of gifts.
4 The poet has respect for her family members.

Stretch zone

Find out about a traditional Chinese celebration, such as the Dragon Boat Festival, the Lantern Festival or the Chinese New Year.

- Match sentences that describe the poems
- Discuss different cultures
- Make an alphabetical list of countries

Talk about a custom or tradition from another country that you know something about. How many different countries do you know? Can you think of a country for each letter of the alphabet?

- Identify structures and features of poems
- Understand how poets form images
- Explain why you prefer one poem to another

B **What do you think?**

Practise reading the poems out loud with a partner.

1 Look at the rhyming words in 'Good Luck Gold'. Which of the lines rhyme? Can you find a pattern?

2 In 'Tea Ceremony', how do we know that the tea tradition was important to Janet's grandfather?

3 Which of the two poems did you like best? Find the words or phrases that helped you decide.

C **What about you?**

Poems can sometimes paint pictures in our minds. Read your favourite of the two poems to yourself again. What pictures does it make you think of?

91

Figurative language (similes, metaphors and alliteration)

Poets often use **figurative language** in their poems. Figurative language can make our work more interesting or dramatic. **Similes** and **metaphors** are two sorts of figurative language. They compare two things in a way that is interesting or even surprising.

Alliteration is also figurative language. Alliteration is when the first consonant sound is repeated in words following each other.

Example: Peter Piper picked a peck of pickled peppers.

A **Which of these sentences are similes and which are metaphors?**

1 Jamila can swim like a fish.
2 Ravi is a scaredy cat.
3 Erik's eyes are as blue as the sky.
4 My best friend is a star.

Stretch zone

Write some similes using these adjectives (clever, tall, cuddly, timid, agile, fearless, scary) and the name of an animal.
Example: as strong as a hippopotamus

- Understand the effect of figurative language
- Write some metaphors, similes and alliteration

B **Fill in the spaces in the sentences using the words below.**

> fast   smiled   flew   slow   light   snail
> blocks of ice   lion   feather   lightning

1 You are as _____ as a _____.
2 Your feet are like _____.
3 You walk as _____ as a _____.
4 He _____ down the street.
5 She was like an angry _____.
6 The sun _____ down on us as we played in the park.

Write one simile and one metaphor describing someone you know.

C **Write alliterative sentences which include a name, an animal and a country all beginning with the same letter. Can you make a sentence for each letter of the alphabet?**

Example: Andy Ant from Australia ate Aunty Anne's apple.

Stretch zone

Write some metaphors to describe a favourite relative. *Example:* Uncle Andrew is a night owl – he stays up all night reading books.

● Read a poem from a different culture

Poetry reading

Poems from different times and cultures

Valerie Bloom is a performance poet. She was born in Jamaica but moved to the UK when she was a young woman. Many of her poems are recalling her memories of growing up in Jamaica.

Granny Is

Granny is
fried **dumplin'** an' **run-dung**,
coconut drops an' **grater cake**,
fresh ground coffee smell in the mornin'
5 when we wake.

Granny is
loadin' up the donkey,
basket full on market day
with fresh **snapper** the fisherman bring
10 back from the bay.

Granny is
clothes washin' in the river
scrubbin' dirt out on the stone
haulin' **crayfish** an' **eel** from the
15 water on her own.

Granny is
stories in the moonlight
underneath the guango tree
and a spider web of magic
20 all round we.

Valerie Bloom

Glossary

dumplin' fried balls of dough

run-dung coconut stew with salted fish

coconut drops/ grater cake sweet desserts made from coconut

snapper type of fish

crayfish/eel freshwater creatures

Comprehension

* Learn how powerful language and rhythm forms images
* Make connections between the poem and real life

This poem is meant to be spoken out loud. Practise saying it with a partner. What do you notice about the rhythm of each verse?

A **Read and respond**

Which two sentences are true?

1 Granny works hard cooking and washing.
2 Granny has no time for her grandchildren.
3 Granny is a good storyteller.

B **What do you think?**

1 Which two words are repeated in each verse?
2 Find the rhyming words. Which lines rhyme in each verse?
3 Which kind of figurative language is used throughout the poem?
   * alliteration
   * simile
   * metaphor
4 Apostrophes have been added to some words to show missing letters. Write out the full words.
   Example: dumplin' = dumpling

C **What about you?**

What adjectives would you use to describe Granny?
Examples: strong, hard-working
Does Granny remind you of anyone in your family? Talk with a partner about memories you have of being with your family members.

95

- Listen to a poem and notice patterns and sounds
- Read the poem
- Analyse the effect of its grammar, punctuation and figurative language

Model poem

This poem is about someone's family tree.
The poet uses lots of different techniques.

My Family Tree

Look, look at my family tree
My family are such an important part of me!

My grandmother
Her smell is of old, fragrant flowers
Her eyes are as sharp as stones
She tells me, "Work hard to succeed."

Kind but razor sharp
My grandmother.

Look, look at my family tree
They are all an important part of me!

My grandfather
His smell is of new tobacco
His hands are like old gloves
He tells me, "Be honest, my son."

Gentle but wise
My grandfather.

- Use a model poem to write your own
- Use a chorus, simile, quotation and contrast
- Use powerful adjectives and verbs

Guided writing

The poet uses techniques including:

1 A chorus, in which lines are repeated.
Example: Look, look at my family tree

2 A simile, which compares one thing to another.
Example: Her eyes are as sharp as stones

3 A quotation.
Example: She tells me, "Work hard to succeed."

4 A line with two contrasting features.
Example: Kind but razor sharp

Writing your own poem

A good way to start writing poetry is to 'copy' another poem. Use the *My Family Tree* poem as a model to write about someone in your family. Change the words so that they suit this person. Remember to copy the same structure and techniques used by the original poet.

Learning tip
When you have written a poem, always read it out loud. Listening to the poem will help you hear how effective the words and phrases are. It will help you to identify which parts of your poem can be improved.

Vocabulary

1   Underline the correct words from the choices below to complete the sentences.

Maya's ancestor was (**an explorer / a mammal**). He understood the (**roots / perils**) of going on expeditions. He had (**hooked / done**) a great deal in his life. Sometimes, he even made the (**headlines / columns**) in newspapers.

Punctuation

1   Copy out this paragraph, adding the apostrophes where they are needed.

There isnt a zoo near us but weve got a park with animals. The keeper is my friends uncle and sometimes he lets us help him. I dont like the iguanas much, but I love the baby kangaroos.

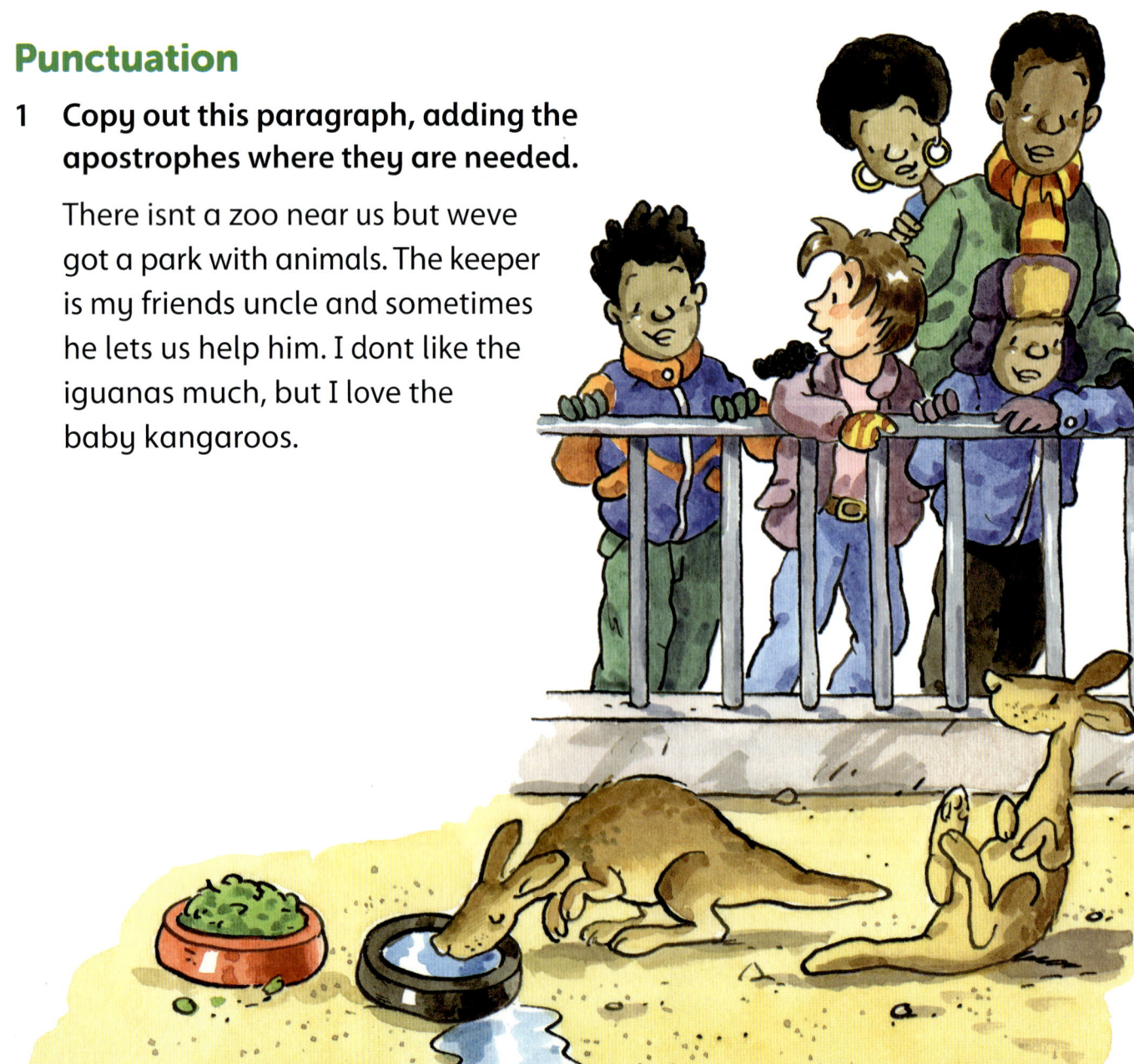

Grammar

1   Divide the phrases in the cloud into similes and metaphors. Make a list like the one here.

Metaphors	Similes
A glowing report	As big as a bus

A dark secret
As white as snow
As cold as ice
Colourful remarks
As busy as a bee
Scaredy cat!
A glowing report
As big as a bus

2   Choose one simile and one metaphor from your list and write a sentence to show their meaning.

3   Read the paragraphs below and complete the sentences with the correct form of the adjective.

African elephants are the **(big)** land animals on the planet! The **(heavy)** elephant weighed 24,000 pounds! They have **(large)** ears than Indian elephants but **(small)** heads and **(few)** toenails.

The **(good)** place to see them is Amboseli in Kenya. They are probably the **(interesting)** animals on the planet!

Spelling

1   Write the comparative form of these adjectives:

gentle   noisy   light   late   tidy

2   Write the superlative form of these adjectives:

early   bad   dirty   loud   sad

7 All together!

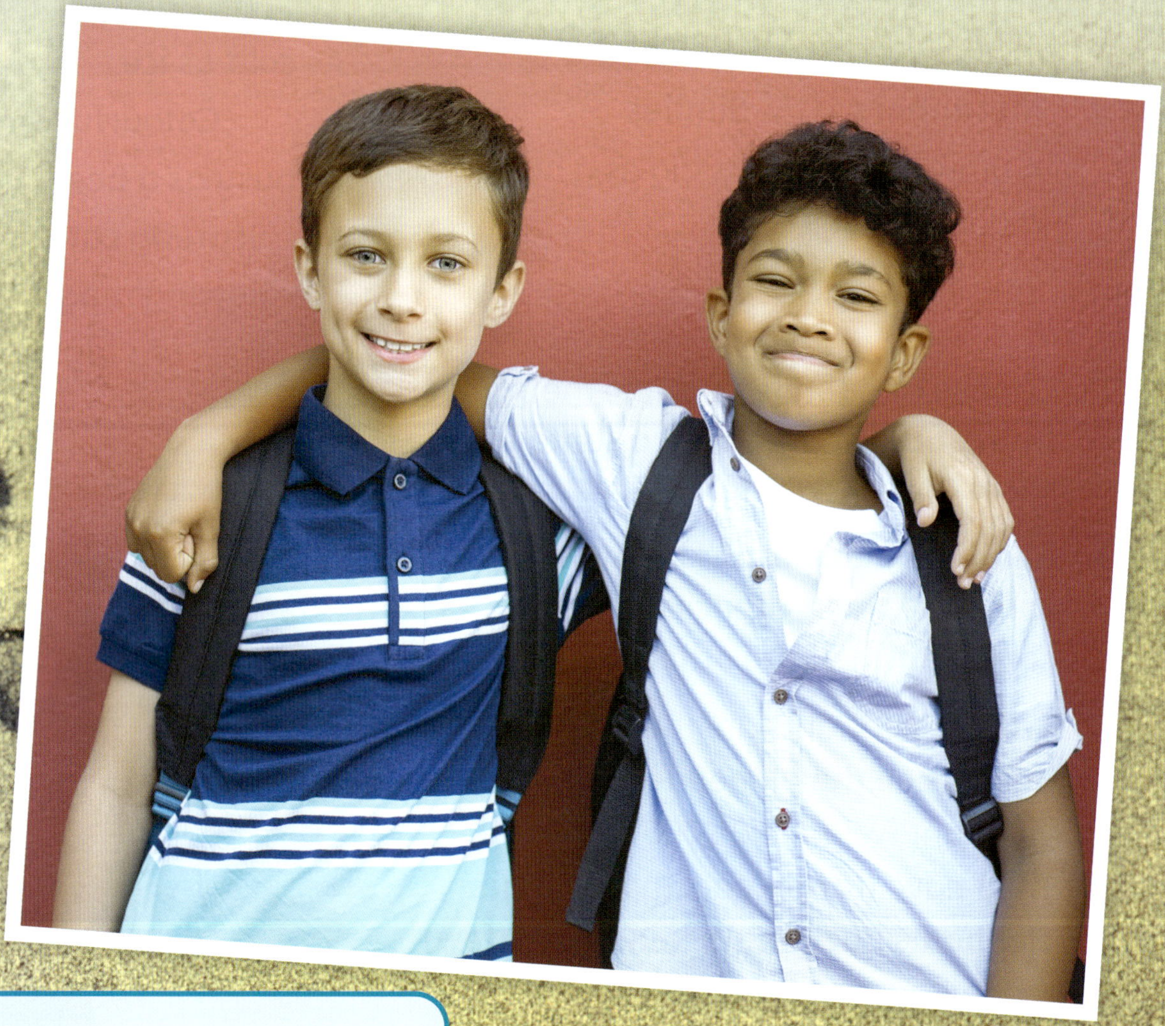

Talk time

1 This picture shows two best friends. In what ways do friends help each other?
2 Think of a time that you helped a friend with a problem, or they helped you. How did you work together to solve the problem?

"Don't walk in front of me; I may not follow. Don't walk behind me; I may not lead. Just walk beside me and be my friend."
Albert Camus

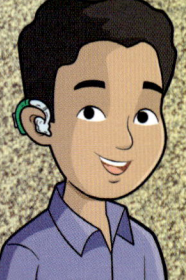

- Join in discussions
- Match words and meanings
- Use synonyms

Thinking about friends

A Work in groups and discuss the following questions.

1 **chum, buddy, mate, pal, ally, companion** are all synonyms for what?
2 Think of the people in your life that you like or love. What qualities do they have that you admire?
3 What do you think the following words mean?

bond   embrace   affection   respect

> **Language tip**
> Synonyms are different words which have the same meaning. *Example:* small and little

B Match the words in activity A1 and A3 with their correct definition. You will not need to use every word.

1 _ _ _ _ a good friend (rhymes with some)
2 _ _ _ _ a special relationship based on shared feelings or experience
3 _ _ _ _ _ _ _ hold someone close in your arms
4 _ _ _ _ _ _ _ to admire good things about someone
5 _ _ _ _ someone who is on the same side as someone else
6 _ _ _ _ _ an American term for good friend
7 _ _ _ _ _ _ _ _ _ a feeling of fondness or liking for someone

C Do you have friends or family members that live in another country? What can you learn from having friends from different places and backgrounds?

Stories about real-life situations

Mona lives in America. Her grandmother lives far away in a small village in the Middle East. Once, Mona went to visit her. They didn't speak the same language, so they made up their own.

Sitti's Secrets

My grandmother lives on the other side of the earth. When I have daylight, she has night. When our sky grows dark, the sun is **peeking** through her window and brushing the bright lemons on her
5 lemon tree. I think about this when I am going to sleep.

"Your turn!" I say…

Once I went to visit my grandmother. My grandmother and I do not speak the same language. We talked through my father, as if he
10 were a telephone, because he spoke both our languages and could **translate** what we said.

I called her **Sitti**, which means Grandma in Arabic. She called
15 me **habibi**, which means darling. Her voice danced as high as the whistles of birds. Her voice giggled and **whooshed** like
20 wind going around corners. She had a thousand rivers in her voice.

From *Sitti's Secrets* by Naomi Shihab Nye

- Listen to and read a story from another culture
- Find information to answer questions
- Discuss ways of communicating

Glossary

peeking quickly and secretly looking at something
translate say in another language
whooshed made a rushing noise, like wind or water

Comprehension

A **Listen and respond.**

Which sentence below is true?

1 Mona and her grandmother live in the same country.
2 Mona doesn't spend time with her grandmother when she visits her.
3 'Sitti' means 'Grandmother'.

B **What do you think?**

Use information from the story to support your answers.

1 What time of day is it for Mona when her grandmother wakes up?
2 Why is Mona's father like a telephone? Explain in your own words.
3 The writer uses metaphors and similes to describe Sitti's voice. Give an example of both from the text.

C **What do you think?**

Mona lives in America and speaks American English. Do you think it is important for Mona to learn her grandmother's language so she can communicate with her relatives from the Middle East?

- Comment on the writer's language choice
- Discuss how a character feels

103

- Listen to and read a story from another culture
- Find information to answer questions
- Explore the writer's language

Stories about real-life situations (continued)

A few curls of dark hair peeked out of her scarf on one side, and a white curl peeked out on the other side. I wanted her to take off the scarf so I could see if her hair was striped.

5   Soon we had invented our own language together. Sitti pointed at my stomach to ask if I was hungry. I pointed to the door to ask if she wanted to go outside. We walked to the fields to watch men picking **lentils**. We admired the sky
10 with hums and claps…

Every day I played with my cousins, Fowzi, Sami, Hani, and Hendia from next door. We played **marbles** together in their courtyard. Their marbles were blue and green and spun through the dust like
15 planets. We didn't need words to play marbles.

From *Sitti's Secrets* by Naomi Shihab Nye

Glossary

lentils type of small bean

marbles game played with small glass balls

A Listen and respond.

Which sentence below is true?
1 Mona can't see any of Sitti's hair.
2 Mona and Sitti are unable to communicate.
3 Mona plays with other children every day.

B **What do you think?**

Read and answer the questions.

1 What does Mona think Sitti's hair looks like? Why does she think this?
2 How do Mona and Sitti communicate with each other? Find examples from the story to support your answer.
3 Why is marbles a good game for Mona to play with her cousins?

C **What about you?**

Do you like the writer's use of language? Explain your answer to a partner and choose three phrases you found particularly effective or interesting.

?

Have you ever been in a similar situation to Mona?
If you didn't speak the same language as someone else, would this stop you being friends?

Stretch zone

Try to communicate with a partner without using words. Did your partner understand what you wanted to say?

- Compare pronouns and possessive pronouns

Pronouns

We use **pronouns** instead of nouns.

- **Pronouns** can be used instead of a person, place or thing.

Pronouns for people: I, you, he, she, it, we, they, me, him, her, us, them.

Pronouns for things: it, they, them.

We use **pronouns** so that we don't keep repeating the same nouns.

Example: I gave Jana an apple because ~~Jana~~ she was hungry.

- **Possessive pronouns** are used to show ownership of a person or thing.

Possessive pronouns: mine, yours, his, hers, ours, theirs

Examples: That book is mine. The book is hers.

Possessive pronouns are used to avoid repetition of the noun. For example:

Jana ate the apple because the apple was hers.

A Find the pronouns. Say whether they are pronouns or possessive pronouns.

1 She tied the child's hair back in a ponytail.
2 The neighbour's house is painted white and so is ours.
3 Don't leave the pens there – put them in the drawer.
4 Asif's phone ran out of battery so he found his charger.

• Identify when to use pronouns and possessive pronouns

B **Replace the words in bold with the correct pronoun.**

1 Amy completed **Amy's** maths homework then packed **the homework** in **Amy's** school bag.

2 Ben's mum said **Ben's mum** had put Ben's lunch in **Ben's** bag to make sure **Ben** didn't forget to take **Ben's** lunch to school.

3 When Jasmine got to school, **Jasmine's** friends told **Jasmine** that **Jasmine's friends** didn't know the answers to the homework.

4 Our house is different to our neighbours' house. **Our neighbours'** house has a pointy roof but **my family's** house is flat.

C **Look at this sentence. Explain why it is not always appropriate to replace a noun with a pronoun.**

Clara gave Jane her bag.

> • Use punctuation and grammar to read with expression

Stories about real-life situations
(continued)

Sitti's Secrets

On the day my father and I had to leave, everyone
cried and cried. Even my father kept blowing his
nose and walking outside. I cried hard when Sitti
held my head against her shoulder. My cousins
5 gave me a sack of **almonds** to eat on the plane.
Sitti gave me a small purse she had made.

People are far apart, but connected. My
grandmother lives on the other side of the
earth. While I am dreaming, she rises
10 from her fluffy bed and steps out
her door to check the lemons
growing on her tree. The
first thing she does every
day is say good morning
15 to her lemons.

All day the leafy shadow of her
tree will grow and change on her courtyard
wall. She will move with its shade. When she
sleeps, she will dream of me.

From *Sitti's Secrets* by Naomi Shihab Nye

Comprehension

- Find answers about characters and events in a story
- Reflect on hidden meaning in a story
- Talk about what you like and dislike in the story

A **Read and respond.**

1 What gifts did Mona receive?
2 What is Sitti doing when Mona is sleeping?
3 What does Mona think Sitti dreams about?

B **What do you think?**

1 How do we know that Mona's father is upset?
2 Did you like the characters in this story? Explain your answer.
3 Whose point of view is this story told from?
   - Sitti
   - Mona
   - a narrator

   Explain how you know.
4 Mona says: 'People are far apart, but connected.' What do you think she means by this?

C **What about you?**

How does the story make you feel? Share your feelings with a partner.

Stretch zone

Which words do you think are the most important words to communicate with?
Example: Yes, please, thank you.
Is it important to use facial expressions (like smiling) when trying to communicate?

Sentence types

A statement is a sentence which ends with a full stop: *Example:* The children are swimming.
A question is a statement which asks something and ends with a question mark: *Example:* Is Lucia from Italy?
An exclamation is a sentence which shows strong feeling and ends with an exclamation mark: *Example:* It's my birthday today!
An order is a sentence which gives a command and sometimes ends with an exclamation mark. Usually an order starts with a verb. *Example:* Shut the door!

A Copy the text and write after each sentence what type it is (statement, question, exclamation or order).

Ali and Tim were fishing by the lake.
"Don't make a noise!" whispered Ali.
"Why?" asked Tim. "Have you caught something?"
"Yes, and it's huge. Oh no! It's a monster!"

B Write the questions to go with these answers. Use words from the box to help you.

> what   where

1 Rattlesnakes live in swamps and forests in America.
2 The students have been learning about rattlesnakes.

Stretch zone

Write a paragraph about working together to solve a problem. Use all four sentence types.

C What kind of sentences are these? Rewrite them as a different type of sentence.

1 Wait behind that tree!
2 Can you hear that noise?

Homophones

Homophones are words that are pronounced in the same way, but have different meanings and often different spellings.
Example: The mother and **son** watched the **sun** go down. They could **see** the **sea**.

- Identify homophones
- Choose a homophone to complete a sentence
- Change incorrect words in a sentence

A Find a homophone for the following words:

> pair   stare   sew   ate   weak

B Choose the correct word to complete the sentence.

1 Who _____ when the bus is coming? (nose/knows)
2 The wind _____ all morning. (blew/blue)
3 There was a _____ in the ground. (hole/whole)
4 She arrived an _____ late. (our/hour)

Learning tip
Keep a list of homophones in your notebook. You can also draw pictures to help you remember what they mean.

C Find the mistake in each sentence. Copy out the sentences, using the correct words.

1 The boy asked for a peace of cake.
2 There were two many cars on the road.
3 The plain arrived on time.
4 My grandparents are very deer to me.

111

Writing a story with an everyday setting
Model writing

Making a Friend

"Good morning, students. Please let me introduce you to our new student." And with that, our head teacher shut the door behind her, leaving us all to look at Jorge Panderez.

He was tall, much taller than anyone else in the class – with a huge mop of black, bushy hair that sat on top of his head like a large hat.

"Hi, everyone," he announced, before walking **casually** to the empty seat beside me. He **thumped** his heavy school bag down and **collapsed** onto the chair. Then he turned to give me a wide grin that **exposed** his two missing front teeth.

At that precise moment, I knew Jorge Panderez and I were going to be best friends.

Glossary

casually in a relaxed way

thumped put something down loudly

collapsed fell suddenly

exposed showed

Guided writing

A good character description will describe what a character looks like, how they move and speak, and how they relate to other characters.

- Describe how a character moves and speaks
- Describe a character's appearance
- Use similes and powerful adjectives

Character features	Examples from the extract
Description of physical features	*Huge mop of black, bushy hair; wide smile with two missing teeth*
How they move	*Walked casually, thumped down his bag, collapsed onto the chair*
How they speak	*He announced*
Relationship with other characters	*Says "Hi, everyone," to the class; smiles at the narrator of the story; the narrator sees him as a best friend*

A good character description will also:

- often use similes.
  Example: 'black, bushy hair that sat on top of his head like a large hat.'
- emphasise a physical feature by repeating it in different ways.
  Example: Jorge's size – 'tall', 'taller', 'huge', 'large'.

Planning a story with an everyday setting

Your writing

Do you have a best friend? Were you best friends from the start or did you become friends over time?

1 Make notes about the time you first met a good friend. Describe:
   - when and where you first saw them
   - what they looked like
   - what they said
   - how they moved
   - how they behaved towards you and others.

2 Use your notes and the success criteria on page 115 to write about the time you first met your friend.

   - Focus only on three or four key physical features, such as size or height, hair and the look on their face.
   - Mention one or two items of clothing they were wearing, but choose your words carefully. Make your description interesting.

Story success criteria

- Plan a story
- Write a character description and setting
- Use success criteria to give and take feedback

When you have finished, swap your description with a partner. Use the success criteria below to give each other feedback.

Success criteria

Does your description include:

- when you first met your friend?

- what they looked like?

- what they said and how they spoke?

- how they moved?

- a time where they proved to be a good friend and helped you?

Have you remembered to:

- use at least one simile?

- use adjectives?

- Check that you have used full stops and capital letters properly and that your spelling is correct.

Stretch zone

Go on to describe a time when your friend proved to be a really good friend.

8 World of water

Talk time

1 What do the two pictures below tell us about water?
2 What title would you give each picture?

"We forget that the water cycle and the life cycle are one."
Jacques Yves Cousteau

Words about water

A Look at the pictures on pages 116 and 117. Which picture shows:

1 a well (a deep hole in the ground where you can get water)

2 somebody drenched (soaked with water)

3 an oasis (a place in a desert with water)

B Look at the brochure (right).

1 Would you like to go to this festival with your friends?

2 How would you persuade your family to take you to this festival?

C 22nd March is World Water Day and schools all over the world organise events to help us remember the importance of water. What would you like your school to do on that day?

Stretch zone

Design a page for a brochure for a family water park with water slides and rides.

COME TO **THAILAND** and CELEBRATE NEW YEAR at the **WATER FESTIVAL** Don't forget to bring a bucket of water or a water gun to drench your friends!

Persuasive text

Protect our Water

The blue planet

About 70% of our planet's surface is covered by water, but most of that water comes from the
5　oceans and is salty, so we cannot drink it.

What water is used for

Humans need to drink water every day to remain healthy. But water has a lot of other uses: we need it to wash our bodies, our clothes and our cars,
10　to cook, water our plants or flush the toilet. On average, a person uses about 140 litres of water per day. And that's nothing compared with the quantity of water used to produce the food we eat or the clothes we wear!

How can we save water?

15 There is a lot we can do to save water; it's all about changing our habits!

- You could have a shower rather than a bath.

20 - Turn off the tap while you are brushing your teeth.

- Make sure the tap is properly turned off after each use because a dripping tap can
25 waste a lot of water.

- If you have a garden, collect rainwater in a water butt and use that for watering your plants.

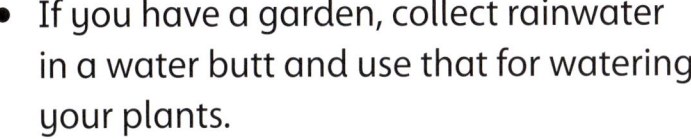

Comprehension

- Find information to answer questions
- Discuss ideas about water waste
- Design a persuasive poster/brochure

A **Listen and respond.**

1 What percentage of the Earth's surface is covered with water?

2 How much water does a person use on average each day?

3 Name four different things we use water for.

B **What do you think?**

1 The article says there is a lot of water on earth. Why is a lot of it not suitable to drink?

2 Did you find any of the facts in the text surprising? If so, which ones and why?

3 Did the text persuade you to use less water? Explain your answer.

4 Is the style of language used in this text different to the tourist brochure on page 117? Describe the different styles.

Stretch zone

Design a system to collect rainwater for watering plants. If you live in a country where there isn't much rain, what else can you do to collect water?

C   What about you?

Do you think it is true that some people are not careful with water? Do you think people would waste less water if they had to collect water from a well?

Design a poster

Design a poster persuading people to use less water. Tell them how important fresh water is but how little there is. Give examples of what people can do to save water. Use the list of tips below to help you.

- Use the present tense.
  Example: Turn off the tap.

- Use bold colours and different sized lettering.
- Use exclamation marks to emphasise urgency.
  Example: Act **NOW** before it's too late!

- Have a catchy title.
  Example: Water you doing to save water?

- Include facts, as well as opinions.
  Example: On average, a person uses about 140 litres of water per day.

- Ask rhetorical questions.
  Example: Can you imagine living in a world with very little water?

- Use linking words to strengthen ideas.
  Example: Water is precious **so** we must take care of it.

?

Sometimes water causes serious problems. Do you think these problems can be avoided? Discuss ideas as a class.

121

Linking words

- Understand that linking words organise ideas
- Choose the right adverbs of time

Explanatory texts often use **subordinating** and **co-ordinating conjunctions** such as **so** and **because** to show cause and effect, and **adverbs of time** such as **then** and **after that** to show the order in which things happen.

Persuasive texts often use **conjunctions** such as **if… so**, **although**, **while** and **because**.

A Copy out these sentences and underline the conjunctions.

1 There is a huge demand for water because there are so many people in the world.
2 Water is precious but some people don't think about the amount they waste.
3 If you run a tap, make sure you turn it off.

B Which three of these words are adverbs of time?

> although   firstly   and
> afterwards   finally   because

Learning tip
Subordinating and co-ordinating conjunctions are often used to help make an argument.

C **Copy and complete these sentences using a conjunction.**

1 Water is precious _____ don't waste a drop! (so, but)
2 All the villagers use the well _____ it has clean water. (although, because)
3 Some people use a hose to clean the car _____ they could use a bucket. (but, and)
4 _____ your friends waste water, persuade them not to! (If, Since)

Stretch zone

Plan an advertisement for an imaginary water-saving product. How will you use linking words to persuade people to buy your product?

IF YOU BUILD THIS WATER WELL, YOU WILL HELP TO SAVE PRECIOUS WATER

The life cycle of a frog

What is a frog?

Frogs are <u>amphibians</u>. That means a frog can live in water or on land. A frog comes from an egg. The frog goes through five different stages of life before it becomes an adult frog. This is known as metamorphosis.

egg ⟶ tadpole ⟶ tadpole with legs ⟶ young frog ⟶ adult frog

Stage 1: egg

A frog starts life as a <u>fertilised</u> egg. A female frog lays lots of eggs in water. The eggs float on the water in a jelly-like substance. This is called frog spawn. The eggs will soon <u>hatch</u> into tadpoles.

Stage 2: tadpole

The newly hatched tadpole doesn't have any legs but does have a long tail. It also has <u>gills</u> that allow it to breathe underwater. For the next few weeks, the tadpole will swim, eat plants from the water, and grow! It will develop <u>lungs</u> so it can breathe out of water.

Stage 3: tadpole with legs

As it grows bigger, the tadpole also begins to grow two back legs to help it swim.

Stage 4: young frog

The tadpole then grows two front legs and its tail begins to disappear. The tadpole uses the <u>nutrients</u> stored in its tail as food. When just a little stub of its tail is left, the tadpole has become a young frog. It hops out of the pond onto dry land for the first time.

Stage 5: adult frog

The frog's tail disappears and the tiny frog now eats insects. For the next 2–4 years it will grow bigger until it is an adult. Then female frogs lay eggs and the whole cycle begins again.

• Summarise by creating a diagram
• Understand new words in context

A Copy this life cycle diagram and complete each stage with the correct picture and explanation.

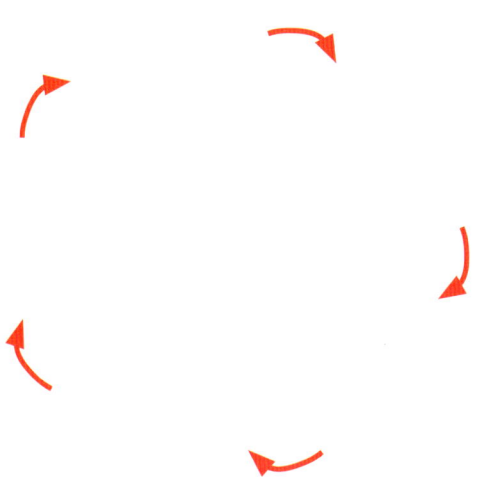

Stages
adult frog
egg
tadpole with legs
young frog
tadpole

B Make a glossary by matching the underlined words in the extract to the correct meaning below.

_____ body part that allows animals to breathe on land

_____ to join sperm with an egg so that a baby or young animal develops

_____ flaps that allow animals such as fish to breathe underwater

_____ break out of an egg

_____ animals that can live on land or in water

_____ something that gives the body what it needs to live and grow

C Match the stage to the changes that take place.

Stage 1   begins to grow back legs
Stage 2   starts to eat bugs
Stage 3   grows two more legs and tail gets shorter
Stage 4   floats on water
Stage 5   looks like a fish

Words with common roots

- Learn about prefixes and suffixes
- Know that adding a prefix or suffix changes the meaning of a word

A **root word** is a word that has meaning even with nothing added to it. It does not have a **prefix** or a **suffix**.

A root word can be used to create lots of different words. We can get clues about the meaning of different words by looking at the root word.

Example: comfort (root word)

suffix	prefix	suffix
comfort**able**	**un**comfort**able**	

Language tip
A prefix comes at the beginning of a word; a suffix comes at the end of the word. Prefixes and suffixes can alter the meaning of the words!

A Copy these bugs. Complete the bugs so that each leg has a word that uses the root word in the centre. Use the prefixes and suffixes in the box to help you.

Prefixes and suffixes
s re ed ing ly
un con de in

B Add a prefix, a suffix or both to the root word shown in brackets to make these sentences correct.

1 The women and girls are (carry) water from the wells (cheerful).

2 The class sang the new song (joy). Their parents (joy) the concert.

3 What an (grateful) man! He didn't thank the (help) children for holding the door open.

C Look at the root words below (left). Explain the new meaning of each word with the added prefix or suffix.

1 act   react
2 behave   misbehave
3 price   priceless
4 pity   pitiful

Writing an explanatory text

Model writing

The water cycle

The water cycle is the journey water takes between the sea, the land and the sky.

5 Then the warmth of the sun makes the water evaporate into water vapour and the cycle begins again.

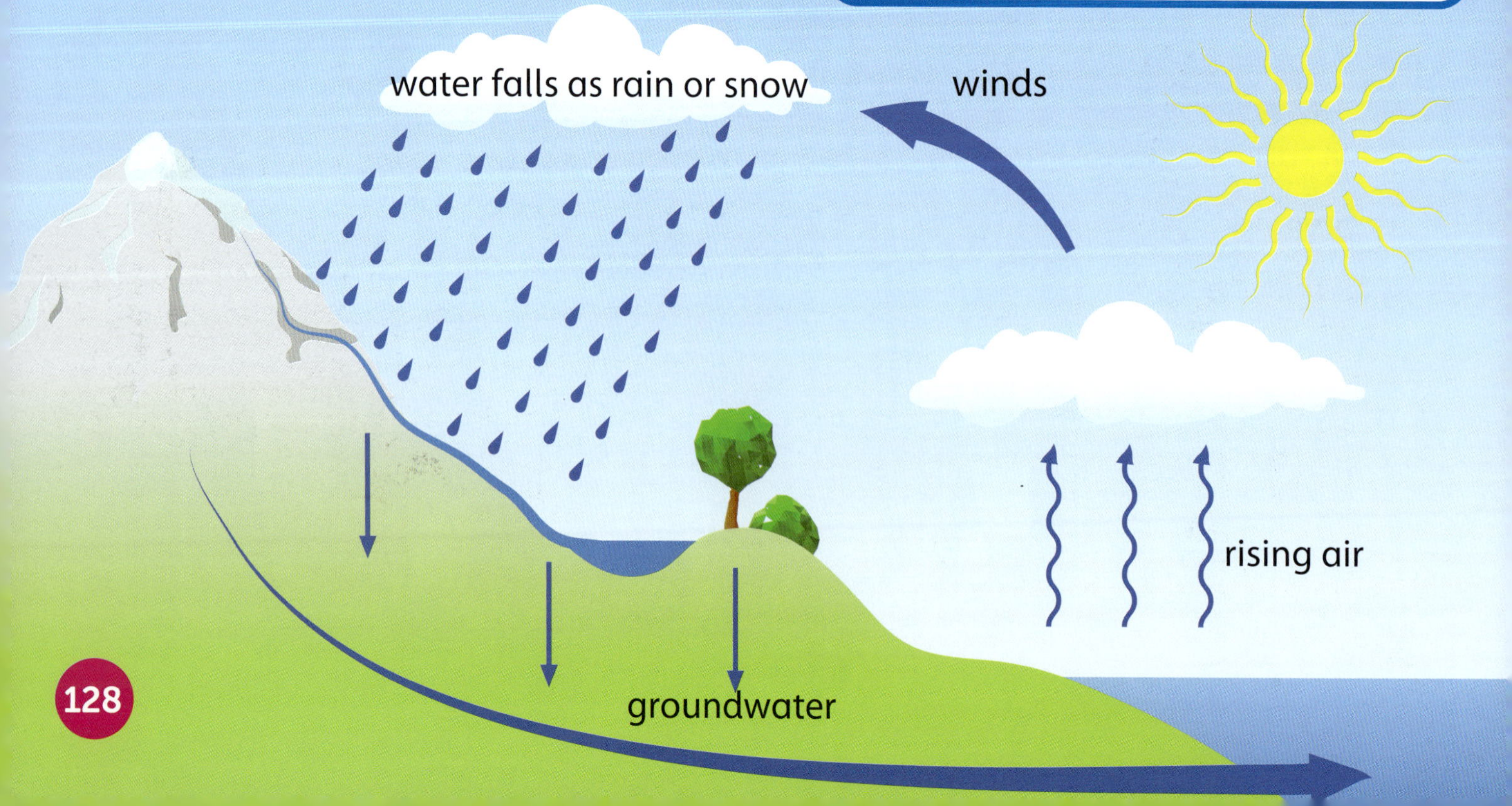

1 Heat from the sun, together with the wind, causes water to evaporate and turn into water vapour (a gas).

4 The rain runs off into streams and rivers, which flow into the sea. It also soaks through the soil. This water is called groundwater.

2 Next, the water vapour rises to the sky. As it cools, it begins to form water droplets, which in turn form clouds.

3 Wind carries the clouds over the land and the water falls as rain or snow.

water falls as rain or snow

winds

groundwater

rising air

Guided writing

An **explanatory text** is similar to a **non-chronological report**.

For example, they both use more formal language. But there are some important differences!

A **non-chronological report** tells us how things are. It is usually organised by topic or theme.

An **explanatory text** explains a process or tells us how something works. It is organised in the order things happen.

- Identify key features of an explanatory text
- Compare an explanatory text and non-chronological report
- Understand paragraphs and adverbs of time

Look at the explanatory texts on pages 124 and 128. Work with a partner. Make a list of all the common features of a explanatory text.

Did you find all of the features listed below?

Common features of an explanatory text

- Has an opening statement that tells the reader exactly what is going to be explained.
- May be presented in paragraphs, with each stage explained in a separate paragraph.
- May be presented as a flow chart, with each stage explained in a separate box.
- Often uses adverbs of time to join ideas.
- May include a labelled diagram.
- Explains difficult words.
- Has a conclusion.

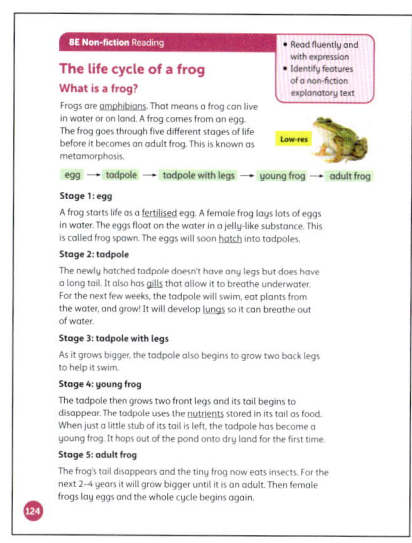

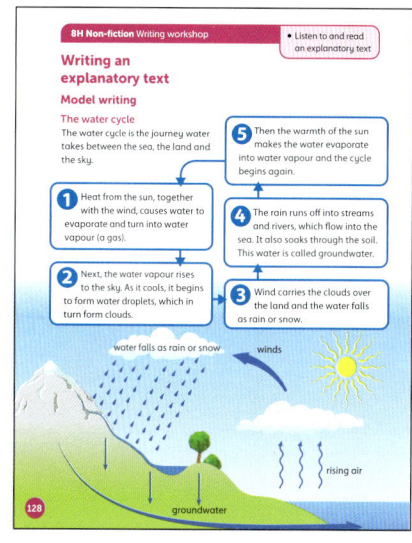

Planning an explanatory text

Making notes

- Decide what your explanatory text is going to be about. The example on page 128 is about the water cycle, but you could write about something else, such as how to make bread or the life cycle of a butterfly.
- Research the process you are going to describe, writing down some key facts.
- Will you present your text in paragraphs or as a flow chart? If you choose paragraphs, make sure each paragraph has a subheading that makes it clear what the paragraph is going to be about.
- Will you need to include a diagram?
- Which difficult words will need to be explained for the reader?

- Find information and take notes
- Plan your explanatory text
- Include the features of an explanatory text

Learning tip

Even if you are going to write in paragraphs, you could make a flow chart first to organise your ideas.

Writing and presentation

Writing

- Use your notes and your list of explanatory text features or the list on page 129 to help you write a rough draft of your explanatory text.
- When you have finished, read your explanatory text out loud. Does the information make sense?
- Swap your text with a partner. Use the success criteria to give them feedback.
- Use your partner's feedback to write a final draft.

- Present information in an easy-to-follow way
- Proofread your writing
- Work with a partner to improve

Presentation

In small groups, take it in turns to read your explanations to each other.

Success criteria

Does your explanatory text:

- begin with a general opening statement?

- divide the stages up into paragraphs or boxes?

- have subheadings for each paragraph?

- have paragraphs or boxes that follow on from the previous one?

- use adverbs of time to link ideas?

- use labelled diagrams or illustrations?

- explain difficult words, i.e. in a glossary?

- have a conclusion, if appropriate?

- Check that you have used full stops and capital letters properly and that your spelling is correct.

9 Poems for all seasons

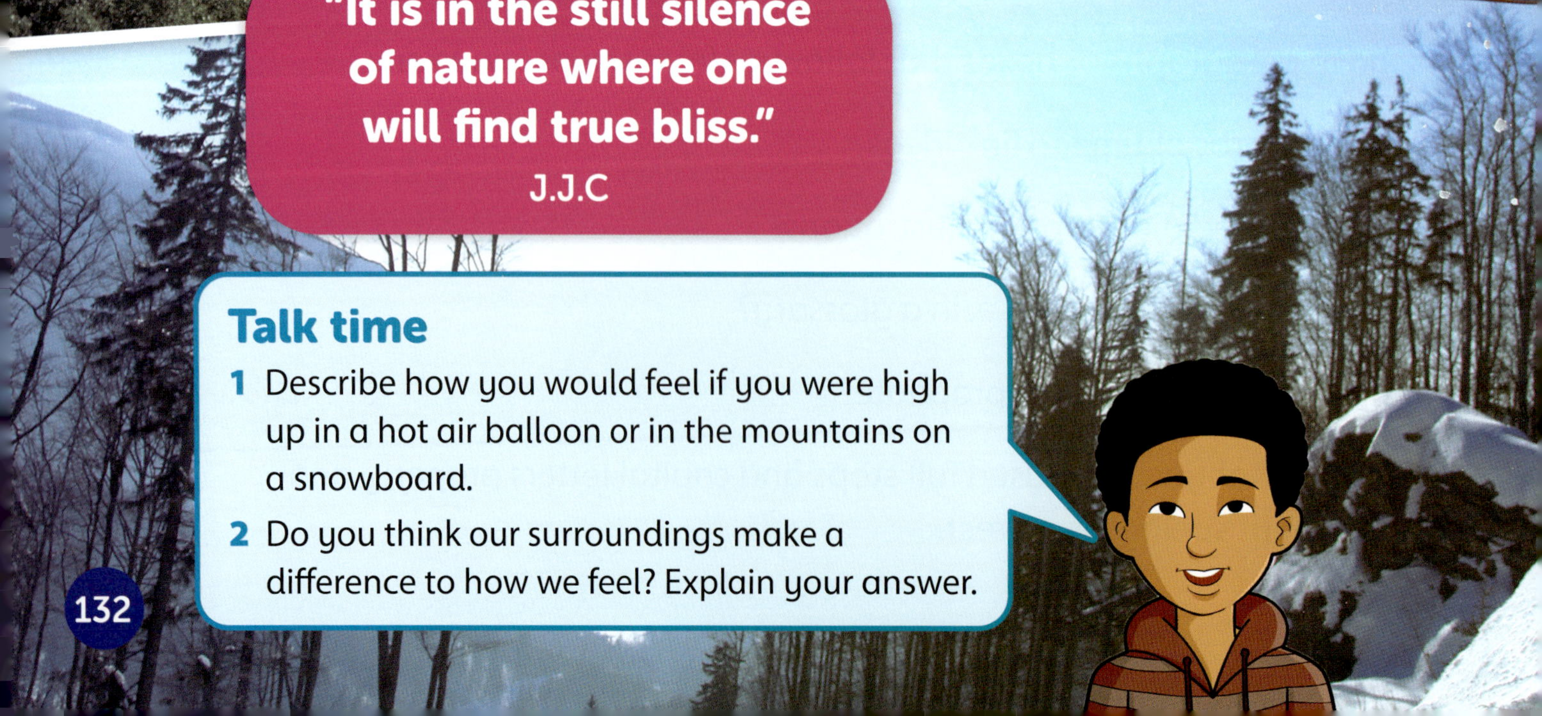

> **"It is in the still silence of nature where one will find true bliss."**
>
> J.J.C

Talk time

1 Describe how you would feel if you were high up in a hot air balloon or in the mountains on a snowboard.

2 Do you think our surroundings make a difference to how we feel? Explain your answer.

Words and syllables

- Find the meaning of unfamiliar words
- Identify and count syllables
- Share ideas with a partner

A Look at the words below and match them to their meaning:

season   shape poem   syllable

1 A word or part of a word with one vowel sound.

2 A poem in which the words are arranged in a special shape.

3 One of the four periods of the year: spring, summer, autumn or winter.

B What do you notice about the number of syllables in this poem?

This
is a
word journey
that started with
just one syllable
on the first lonely line,
but then increased to two, and
added one more with each new line
until the writer decided that
the journey's end should be at number ten.

Mike Jubb

C Which is your favourite season? Think of words of one, two and three syllables to describe it. Share your words with a partner.

• Learn about different types of poems

Different forms of poems

A **haiku** is a poem of three lines with the syllable pattern 5, 7, 5.

A **cinquain** is a poem of five lines with the syllable pattern 2, 4, 6, 8, 2.

A **tanka** is a poem of five lines with the syllable pattern 5, 7, 5, 7, 7.

Cinquain

Cold rain
Falling **fiercely**
We are like **stranded** fish
Splashing through wet,
    grey streets swimming
For home

Haiku

An old silent pond...
A frog jumps into the pond,
splash! Silence again.

Matsuo Bashō, translated by Harry Behn

Tanka

Wind **rustles** gently
In almost **bare** trees, waiting.
The sky threatens rain
Then a quick burst of sunlight
And a rising **skylark** sings.

Glossary

fiercely strongly
stranded left in a place that you can't leave
rustles sound like paper or dry leaves moving
bare naked, empty, without leaves
skylark bird

Shape poem
Sun

Go to sleep,
SUNSET.

Wake up,
SUNRISE.

Sad and angry,
SUNBURN.

Squint and blink,
SUNBEAM.

Summer fun,
SUNLIGHT.

Summer plants,
SUNFLOWER.

Laugh and play,
SUNSHINE.

Tell the time,
SUNDIAL.

Mary-Luz Espiritusanto

Comprehension

- Learn how poems are constructed
- Discuss words or phrases you like

A Read and respond

1 What topics do the different poems have in common?

2 Three of the poetry forms follow a particular syllable pattern. Which one does not?

3 Find an example of **alliteration** in one of the poems.

4 Find an example of a **simile** from one poem and a **metaphor** from another poem.

B What do you think?

1 How much time has passed from the start of the shape poem to the end?

2 Which words or phrases in the poems did you find most effective?

3 Did you dislike any of the poems? Give reasons for your answer.

Stretch zone

The haiku on page 134 was written by Matsuo Bashō, a very famous Japanese poet. Do some research to find out more about him and read more of his haiku.

?

Many poets are inspired by nature and the changing of the seasons. They see things that give them new ideas and make them want to write. What do you find inspiring in nature? Share your ideas in a small group.

- Write five words about nature

C What about you?

Get some inspiration for a nature poem of your own! Choose one of the places below and one of the seasons. Imagine you are in that place in that season. What can you see, smell and feel? Write five descriptive words that come into your mind.

Spring   Summer

Autumn   Winter

desert

beach

woodland

mountain

river

hill

137

- Recognise different sounds made by the same spelling

Same letters, different sound

Some words contain the same letters in the same order, but we pronounce the words differently. Look at these words, which all contain the letter string **ear**. Say the words aloud. What do you notice?

le**ar**n

ear

b**ear**

h**ear**t

A Sort these words into three groups that have the same sound.

wear	fear	bear
year	earn	heard
early	pear	beard

● Learn to spell/say words with common letter strings

B Which word in the cloud has the same sound as the word in the sun?

tough

cough rough
through

rice

police nice
practice

shout

journey four
without

Stretch zone

Think of four more words with the **oo** letter string – two with the **oo** sound in 'mood' and two with the **oo** sound in 'book'.

C Which words with the **oo** letter string complete this rhyming poem?

If I'm in the m**oo**d
to eat some nice _____.
I look in a b**oo**k
and ch**oo**se what to _____!

- Read and analyse types of poems

Different forms of poems (continued)

A **performance poem** is meant to be spoken out loud.

A **limerick** is a funny poem of five lines.

A **riddle poem** is a puzzle set out as a poem.

Glossary

vale/dale valley

moor area covered in rough grass

ditch long, narrow hole to hold or take away water

brute unpleasant animal

Performance poem

Fruit Picking

Raspberry, strawberry, gooseberry, plum,
Fruit picking time is really good fun;
Out in the field, in our hats, in the sun,
Raspberry, strawberry, gooseberry, plum.

Gooseberry, strawberry, raspberry, plum,
Carefully picking with finger and thumb;
When the baskets are full our picking is done,
Gooseberry, strawberry, raspberry, plum.

Raspberry, gooseberry, strawberry, plum,
Here is a tune for pickers to hum;
Tap out the beat like the sound of a drum,
Raspberry, gooseberry, strawberry, plum.

Raspberry, strawberry, gooseberry, plum,
Now in our beds when night-time has come
We can think of our wonderful day in the sun,
Raspberry, strawberry, gooseberry, plum.

Jack Ousbey

Riddle

My first is in water, but isn't in air,

My second's in ocean and sea, but not there.

My third's in a river but not in a **vale**,

My fourth is in stream, but not **moor**, hill or **dale**.

My fifth can be seen in a **ditch** – not a street –

And my whole can be found under everyone's feet.

Alison Chisholm

Limerick

There was an Old Man in a Tree

There was an Old Man in a tree,
Who was horribly bored by a bee;
When they said, "Does it buzz?"
He replied, "Yes, it does!"
"It's a regular **brute** of a bee!"

Edward Lear

Comprehension

A **Which sentences below are true?**

1 A limerick has no rhyme or rhythm.
2 A performance poem often has repetition and rhythm.
3 A riddle poem is like a puzzle that you have to work out.

B **What do you think?**

1 Which pairs of words in 'Riddle' rhyme?
2 Do you think a performance poem has a pattern or structure? Explain your answer.
3 Which of the three poems did you like the most and why?

C **What about you?**

The poem 'Fruit Picking' describes the poet's memories of a wonderful day in summer. Compare the poet's image of summer with summer in the country you live in. What would be your idea of a wonderful day in summer? Discuss your ideas with a partner.

- Compare poems
- Decide which you prefer and why
- Discuss ideas with a partner

Stretch zone

With a partner, choose one of the poems in the unit. Practise saying it out loud. Decide whether you will recite the whole poem together or take separate lines. Practise your expression and tone until you are ready to perform your poem in front of the class.

- Listen to the rhythm and language of a list poem

Model poem

List poem

Spring is in the Air

spring cleaning,
spring planting,
spring pruning,

bees,
butterflies,
allergies,

campfires,
marshmallows,
smores,

spring break,
school is out soon,
happy tired children,

the smell of flowers,
fresh spring rain,
first mowed grass,

just a few of my favourite things!

Karen Croft

Stretch zone

Can you find some examples of words in the poem which share the same letters but make a different sound, like 'bear' and 'learn'?

Guided writing

A list poem uses a list structure. Choose one season of the year. Make a list of words and short phrases to describe it. Think about what you:

do see hear smell taste feel

Try to structure your ideas in groups of three, like 'Spring is in the Air'.

Writing your own poem

1 Use the structure of 'Spring is in the Air' to write your own list poem. Use the list of things you can do in your chosen season.
Example:
Summer: swimming, surfing, barbecuing
Then add some of your other ideas describing what you do and how you feel. Remember to keep your ideas in groups of three.

2 Read your poem out loud to a partner. Do they agree with your syllable count for each line? Which line of the poem did they like best, and why? Is there anything you can change to make it better?

3 Practise saying your poem out loud again. Remember to vary your intonation and tone and add hand or facial gestures where appropriate.

4 Hold a class poetry reading session.

- Use the model poem to write your own list poem
- Share feedback with a partner
- Compare the poems in the unit and perform one

Language tip
List poems don't need to rhyme, but they do need a rhythm. Try to use the same number of syllables in each line as the model poem.

Revise and check ③

Vocabulary

1 Complete the sentences with these words:

> waste   oasis   syllables   fluffy

a The clouds are white and _____ .
b How many _____ are in a haiku poem?
c Don't _____ water.
d Look, an _____ at last!

> whooshed   well   demand   drenched

e Oh no, Anna, you're _____!
f The wind _____ across the hills.
g Is there a growing _____ for water?
h Keep away from the _____ – it's dangerous!

Punctuation

1 Look at the sentences in the vocabulary exercise above.

a Which of the sentences are questions?
b Which of the sentences are statements?
c Which of the sentences are exclamations?
d Which of the sentences are orders?

Describe the punctuation that is needed for each type of sentence.

Grammar

1 Divide the words below into families and write them in columns with the root word at the top.

> agreed   unhelpful   clearing   helping
> cleared   helps   disagree   unclear   agreement

2 Find the adverbs in this word snake and write a list.

3 Use the adverbs from the word snake to join these sentences. You can also use 'and'.

a Check your local weather report. Make sure there is enough wind to fly kites!

b Find a large open area. Hold the kite in both hands. Toss it into the wind.

c Keep an eye on your kite. Sometimes the wind changes direction and the kite can crash.

d Bring the kite down. Slowly wind the kite string around a spool.

Spelling

1 Copy out the sentences below using the correct word.

a Granny came to stay for a (**weak/week**).

b He carried the bag of (**flour/flower**) into the kitchen.

c Meet me under the (**pear/pair**) tree.

d The boy (**blue/blew**) out all the candles on the cake.

e Don't forget to (**weight/wait**) for your sister!

A Tale of Gold and Frogs

Long ago, before you or I were born, two sisters lived in a small cottage at the foot of the mountains. The younger was called Cathleen and the elder was called Noreen. Although they were sisters, they were as different as night and day.

One morning, Cathleen set off for a walk, following the path that led into the mountains. After a while, the ground became rockier and Cathleen came across a cave that she'd never noticed before. Inside, she saw four old women sitting in the **flickering** light of a fire. They were dressed in long robes with woven **garlands** on their heads.

"Welcome, Cathleen. We're glad you've come," said one of the women. "Come in and sit by the fire."

Cathleen thanked them and sat down.

Glossary

flickering burning or shining unsteadily
garlands flowers worn as a decoration

"Now we have a question for you," said the old woman. "What do you think of the seasons of the year?"

Cathleen smiled. "Ah, that's easy to answer. To start with there's spring, when nature bursts into life. There are buds on the trees and wild flowers in the woods. I always think that spring is full of promise."

Glossary

content happy

"So it is, Cathleen. So it is," said the old woman, sitting back with a satisfied smile.

"Then there's summer," Cathleen went on. "The days are long and the sun is warm. Sometimes I lie in the grass or cool my feet in the stream. I think that everyone loves the summer."

"So they do, Cathleen. So they do," said the second old woman, also sitting back, **content**.

"After that comes autumn, when the trees turn red, **copper** or golden," said Cathleen. "We have **bonfires** and there are apples and berries to bake in pies. I always think that autumn is a wonderful time."

"So you do, Cathleen. So you do," said the third old woman with a smile.

"And last there's winter," said Cathleen. "The days are shorter but in the evening I can sit and read or sew by the fire. Sometimes the fields are frosty or thick with snow, so I think winter is a beautiful season. To be honest, I'd say I'm happy with every season of the year!"

"So you are, Cathleen. So you are," said the fourth old woman, nodding and sitting back like the others.

> ### Glossary
>
> **copper** reddish-brown colour
>
> **bonfires** large fires lit outdoors

Then she spoke again. "You have answered us well, Cathleen, and in return we'd like to give you a **reward**. Reach out and take some coals from the fire and fill your apron."

Of course, Cathleen knew very well you should never touch hot coals. But, to her surprise, when she scooped one up in her apron, it didn't **scorch** the cloth or her fingers at all.

She thanked the old women for their kindness, and then hurried back down the mountain the way she'd come.

When she reached the cottage she called out, "Noreen, Noreen, come and see what I have!"

Her sister came running downstairs. Imagine Cathleen's surprise when she tipped out her apron, for instead of coals, a shower of gold coins tumbled out onto the floor!

Glossary

reward something given to a person in return for something they have done
scorch burn

When Noreen heard the whole story she was eaten up with **envy**. *Why should my sister get all the luck?* she thought. *I'll go up the mountain myself and get my share.*

The next morning she put on the biggest apron she could find and climbed the path. Soon she found the cave, exactly as Cathleen had described it. The four old women were sitting around their fire, just as before.

"Welcome, Noreen," one of them said. "We're glad you've come."

Noreen sat down by the fire without waiting to be asked. "Right. You'll be wanting to know what I think of the seasons of the year," she said. "Well, I'll keep it short. First, there's spring: a terrible, nasty season. One moment it's raining and windy, and then the next it's sunny. I'm cleaning and dusting all day long, so I don't like spring at all."

"So you don't, Noreen. So you don't," said the first old woman, sitting back with a frown.

Glossary

envy a feeling that you want what someone else has

Noreen went on without pausing for breath. "Summer's no better. It's too hot and my skin is too pale for me to sit in the sun. There are flies and wasps and the milk turns **sour**. I sometimes think that summer's the worst of all."

"So you do, Noreen. So you do," said the second old woman, sitting back with a shake of her head.

"As for autumn! Where to start?" grumbled Noreen. "There are leaves in the yard and apples on the trees that all need picking. I do nothing but work and cook all day, which puts me in an awful mood."

"So it does, Noreen. So it does," sighed the third old woman, folding her arms.

"That leaves winter, which nobody likes," **moaned** Noreen. "It's cold and dark and my boots get all muddy. Even with a blanket I'm frozen half to death at night. So I think all the seasons are as bad as each other."

"And so you do, Noreen. So you do," agreed the last old woman, sitting back with the others.

Then she spoke again. "Well, you have answered us truthfully, and in return we'd like to give you a reward."

Noreen didn't wait to be asked. She bent down and filled her big apron with as many coals as she could carry. Then she left without a word of thanks and hurried back down the mountain path.

When she reached the cottage she cried out, "Cathleen, Cathleen, come and see what I have!"

Glossary

moaned complained or grumbled

But Noreen's look of **triumph** soon turned to horror, for instead of gold coins, what came tumbling from her apron was a shower of green frogs! They hopped and jumped everywhere, landing on tables and in teacups. Noreen chased them through the house with a broom, stamping and **howling** with **fury**.

For all I know, she's still complaining about them to this very day.

Alan MacDonald

Glossary

triumph a feeling of winning or success

howling crying loudly like an animal

fury very strong anger

The White Seal

Kotick's mother knew he was special from the moment she saw him. It took the other seals a little longer to realise.

There were a number of white seals born every year, but their coats all darkened rapidly in their first weeks of life. Kotick's fur stayed as white as a **foaming** wave. To begin with, the others were a little afraid of Kotick, but as he grew and played and learned like all the others they soon accepted his strange whiteness.

It wasn't just the way he looked that was different, though. While his friends learned to catch fish the way seals always had, Kotick experimented with new methods. When they were taught how to sleep on their backs in the open ocean, the others chattered and giggled and **nodded off** while Kotick gazed up at the stars and wondered why seals existed, and whether they could change their **destinies**.

> ### Glossary
>
> **foaming** having lots of bubbles on water
> **nodded off** fell asleep
> **destinies** things that will happen

And as the years passed, it became time for Kotick and his friends to fight one another for the best resting grounds on the beach they made their home every summer. As the strongest won the biggest, cleanest rocks and the weakest were forced to make do with patches that were **clogged** with plastic bottles, Kotick set his sights on a far greater prize.

He looked around him at the fighting seals and the dirty swirls of plastic junk. What if there were a place somewhere that was protected from all this rubbish that humans tipped into the oceans?

Glossary

clogged full and blocked

honing improving

Clean water, a wide empty beach, flat rocks, good fishing. The thought burrowed down into Kotick's mind like a sand crab, and never let go.

He mentioned the idea to his father, who told him to stop being silly and focus on **honing** his fighting skills.

He talked to his friends, who just laughed at him as if he had suggested that the world was round.

155

Undeterred, he sought out Great Walrus and found him sleeping, his huge, blotchy body half in and half out of the water, on a rocky **islet** half an hour's swim from the beach.

"Walrus!" Kotick shouted, bobbing cheerfully in the water. "Wake up!"

"What is it, you prickly little sea urchin?" Great Walrus grumbled.

"I have decided to find a beach for the seals to use in summer that is untouched by human rubbish. Where should I look?"

Great Walrus blew loudly through his nostrils. "Such a place does not exist in all the ocean. Their junk is everywhere now. But if you are determined to look, you might first speak with Old Sea Cow."

"She's the only thing in the sea uglier than Great Walrus!" screeched a low-flying gull.

Great Walrus said no more, just rolled over a few times and settled back to sleep, his **bristly** chin resting on a small rock.

In October, it was time for the seals to leave the beach and go their separate ways through the deep ocean in small groups. Kotick's mother taught him to perfect his hunting skills, and by the end of winter there was nothing he did not know about catching fish.

"Now you must become an adult," said Kotick's father one day. "You must make your own way through the ocean, alone, and come to the beach in summer by yourself."

So Kotick rubbed noses with his parents and swam away with one thing on his mind.

Everywhere he went he asked about Old Sea Cow, until one morning Kotick awoke, in **shallow** water, and saw that a dark shadow had appeared overnight on the sea bed nearby, like a mass of seaweed.

But it didn't move like seaweed. Slowly it swayed in Kotick's direction, until he saw that it had **stumpy** flippers, and the most wrinkled, whiskery face imaginable.

Glossary

shallow not deep
stumpy short

"Sea Cow!" Kotick began. "I need your help. Where in the world is there a beach that seals can find in summer, but human rubbish cannot?"

Old Sea Cow said nothing, just turned and drifted away across the sea bed, **beckoning** with a flipper.

So Kotick followed Old Sea Cow across the ocean, swimming slowly and steadily, until she suddenly sped up, heading for the coast and a sheer cliff that sliced down straight into the sea.

Down sank Old Sea Cow, and Kotick with her. She led the young seal to a hole in the cliff like a tunnel. The young seal felt a sharp prickle of fear as all light was **snuffed** out by the rock surrounding him.

> **Glossary**
>
> **beckoning** waving someone over
> **snuffed** put out

By the time they resurfaced on the other side of the cliff, Kotick's lungs were bursting, and he broke the surface of the water gasping for air.

His gasps turned to **gleeful** laughter soon enough when he saw the smooth rocks, the wide beach, the clean sand and the thick **shoals** of fish glittering beneath.

Sheltered from the open sea and accessed through an underwater tunnel, the water and beach held not the tiniest sign of human junk.

So after he had thanked Old Sea Cow, and checked that the fishing was good, Kotick swam back out and headed across the ocean to the seals' summer beach, where all the other seals had already found and fought for their patches for the season.

At first, they did not believe him when he told of the **pristine** new beach he had found, but some eventually agreed to follow him and see for themselves. Of course when they saw it they came back to the other seals in a state of great excitement, until the whole beach was **abandoned**, and all the seals had moved to Kotick's new beach.

Glossary

gleeful happy
shoals groups of fish
pristine not spoilt
abandoned left behind

They still fought for the best spots on the beach, but they were happy with their clean new home, and Kotick was **hailed** a hero for the rest of his days. And ever since, seals everywhere have told their children about the Great White Seal who thought for himself and explored new coasts and did it all for his people.

Benjamin Hulme-Cross

Glossary

hailed named, known as